Uncivil War

poems

Indran Amirthanayagam

Cover design by Anandan Amirthanayagam

Amirthanayagam, Indran, author
    Uncivil war / Indran Amirthanayagam.

Poems.
ISBN 978-1-927494-23-3

    1. Sri Lanka – History – Civil War, 1983-2009 – Poetry.
I. Title.

PS8601.M57U53 2013   C811'.6   C2013-903557-5

Acknowledgements

Some of these poems were published in earlier versions in:

www.groundviews.org, *The Times of India, Transcurrents, Mascara, Wasafiri, Memewar, Napalm Health Spa, Hanging Loose, Rattapalax, The Sunday Times* (Sri Lanka), *MOCAD,* and http://indranamirthanayagam.blogspot.com.

Printed and bound in Canada by Coach House Printing.

TSAR Publications
P. O. Box 6996, Station A
Toronto, Ontario M5W 1X7
Canada
www.tsarbooks.com

This is my life, poetry, the island where I was born, and which I have left, not of my own volition, led by the unseen hand and the dilemmas faced by my parents who saw in exile and abroad a chance for their children to live and grow happily and in peace. We have gone back to Ceylon and will return again, in poems and with our hearts beating, on our own feet.

This book belongs to all its readers, to all who have helped us along the way, who opened their homes and hearts, who fed and clothed and inspired us to become citizens of cricket and mangos and unleavened bread, of all the continents and some of its beloved languages, of mathematics and art, of dance, of the idea that poetry does make something happen, goes far beyond the valley of its saying.

Thank you. Gracias. Obrigado. Merci. Istuti. Nandri.

INDRAN AMIRTHANAYAGAM

Contents

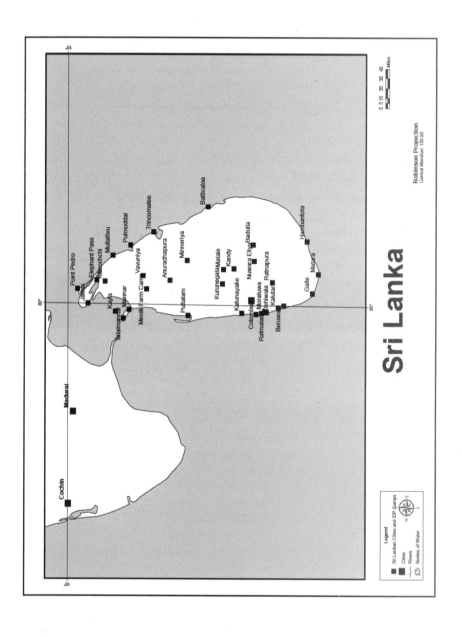

Sri Lanka

Robinson Projection
Central Meridian: 100.00

0 5 10 20 30 40 Miles

Legend
■ Sri Lankan Cities and IDP Camps
■ Cities
〰 Rivers
🔷 Bodies of Water

Point Pedro
Jaffna
Elephant Pass
Kilinochchi
Mullaitivu
Pulmoddai
Trincomalee
Batticaloa
Kayts
Mannar
Talaimannar
Merial Farm Camp
Vavuniya
Anuradhapura
Minneriya
Hambantota
Kurunegala
Matale
Kandy
Nuwara Eliya
Badulla
Putlalam
Katunayake
Ratnapura
Mataraa
Galle
Colombo
Moratuwa
Ratmalana
Dehiwala
Kalutar
Beruwala

Madurai

Cochin

Foreword

Ah, what an age it is
When to speak of trees is almost a crime
For it is a kind of silence against injustice.
                    "To Posterity," BERTOLT BRECHT

I curate a citizen journalism website in Sri Lanka called Ground-
views. It is an effort anchored to a strong belief in bearing witness
to violence. The site celebrates and cultivates dissent through prose,
verse, audio, video, and still photography. In 2009, Groundviews
invited renowned Sri Lankan writers to respond creatively to the
overarching violence, the vicious clampdown on freedom of ex-
pression in Sri Lanka. Indran was one of those who responded.

I first met Indran at the Galle Literary Festival in January 2008,
where he launched and read from his new collection of poetry,
Splintered Face Tsunami Poems. This collection is a sublime example
of an imaginative power and quiet resolve able to transcend a more
parochial violence. Primarily through wit and imagination, a poet's
turn of phrase can focus attention to that which is hidden, forgotten
or marginal. It is not often that poetry influences politics, though
arguably politics in all its forms undergirds the creation and appre-
ciation of poetry. Indran's verse, however, is different and powerful
because as Adrienne Rich notes in *Blood, Bread, and Poetry: The Loca-
tion of the Poet,*

> We fear poetry, because it might persuade us emotionally of what we
> think we are rationally against; it might get to us on a level we have
> lost touch with, undermine the safety we have built for ourselves,
> remind us of what is better left forgotten.

It is this subversive power that poetry alone can offer when other
media are censored, and prose curtailed. Sadly, we have seen this in
our country. Sri Lanka's final stage of war resulted in casualties well
beyond the theatre of military operations in the north and east of
the country. Independent media and investigative journalism were

silenced. In this war without witness, atrocities were committed by both the LTTE and the Sri Lankan Army. This was a war won on the ground, but a battle was lost for the rights of Tamils, whose aspirations and legitimate grievances remain as marginalized as they were before.

The poems in the following pages are obviously partial, and subjective, incomplete brushstrokes on a canvas framed by Indran's own situation. It is certainly possible to critique Indran's focus, partial to Tamils. In the following pages, we do not often see a critical scrutiny of the LTTE and its mind-boggling violence, often against Tamil children, women, and men. Yet the poet makes no excuses for this, and is no apologist. It is a delicate balance. Indran is unafraid of writing from the contested space of the marginal, the violated and the victimized. In other words, a more general commentary of violence is eschewed for a perspective—never once projected as the sole or only truth—from within Indran's understanding of himself as fundamentally a Tamil, and all that meant and means in Sri Lanka. There is, for example, the recognition of a deeper humanity transcending the terrible violence of Sri Lanka's exclusive ethnic communities. In "Riot" the poet writes about friends who helped protect his father though this is never mentioned, they were obviously Sinhalese:

When the mob
assembled
in the plaza
outside

the Law Courts,
at the Galle Fort,
1958, friends
spirited

the Assistant
Government
Agent, my future
father, out

of its hands.

Without friends,
he would not
have lived.

This sort of humanity resonates in Indran's verse, even when informed and framed by anger and grief. Poems on Neelan Thiruchelvan and Manik Sandrasagara bring this out the best. On the other hand, writing about the murder of Lasantha Wickremetunge, editor of the *Sunday Leader*, the poet does not mince his words. In "Murder Investigation: Interview," based on an infamous and outrageous interview given by a senior government official soon after the murder, the poet crafts verse using the heinous wordplay heard on-screen.

Parts I and II of this collection deal with Sri Lanka's war. It is visceral, resonant and touches a chord many would like silenced; it wrenches the gut. Poems like "Smoke Signal" and those on Puthukudiyiruppu Hospital take us back to the time of the bloody denouement, and the collateral deaths. We see an unnerving prescience in "Question of Arms Sales,"

War on Terror,
once declared,
is permanent,
impossible
conceptually

to remove
from psyche
and language.

Part III is also dark, but the issues are mundane. In "Parental Concerns," for example, we see the poet as a caregiver:

other worries, now,

my son and
daughter,
they require time,
not poetry,
or island thuggery.

A foreword is not the place to critique the poet's expression and selection. Indran the poet, the father, the diplomat, the Tamil, the expatriate, the Sri Lankan, my friend, is flawed, like I am, and we all are. Indran asks us in this volume to find our own way out of hell, and in addition to gods and preachers, to use poetry to this end. His own poetry offers no easy escape. It forces us to confront, remember, and acknowledge. If it forces us to refute, to disclaim, to decry and denounce, it still compels us to see anew. I do not see Sri Lanka through Indran's chiaroscuro of hope and despair, but I do recognize his country as my own, loved first and the most.

SANJANA HATTOTUWA

I. Before

AFLAME
Remembering Black July, 1983

What is a poem
to a man hiding
in the cellar
of his neighbor's house,

breathing the way
his hostess spices
lentils and mutton,
while son and daughter

keep quiet,
not one word
allowed
in the mother tongue,

and wife strokes
her neck,
the golden wings
of her thali,

and across the lane
a mob, ruffians,
tontons macoutes,
lynch squad, a few

holy men, politicians
in white vershtis,
light rage
and sow pestilence

in summer fires
that turn houses
to foundation stones
and stoke residents

out to shelter
at neighbors,
St. Peter's College,
the police station

near Bambalapitya Flats,
before three days
voyage on a ship
hungry to Kankesanthurai

where soldiers
have been swinging
cricket bats
and teenage boys

have stopped
playing cricket,
disappeared,
coerced

into resistance:
this war, these
flames burning
every day since,

and even before,
fifty years ago,
1958, when mobs
first enforced

what was deemed
the people's will
by unleashing
latent and dark

social energies,
microbes that murder,

that insist on power
as well as alms,

that circulate
in the body politic
and can only
be diffused,

diverted,
distracted, educated,
burned
out of existence

so Ceylon
may take a bow,
step out
of retirement,

save the side
with sixes,
and at the
victory party

speak of boar
and partridge,
gotukola and
other medicinal

greens, traits
of the veddah,
and how
good neighbors

gave food
gave shelter
denied
the goondas?

ADOPTED CAT

The headline announces
a two-hundred-and-forty-five pound tiger
wandered out of his cage
at the Honolulu Zoo.

A vague disquiet
and blinding joy
overwhelm my mind
and body. Inevitably

I think of all tigers
who have snarled
out of pages
of poetry. Shall

I call them to order
for new readers?
The Other Tiger
Borges invented

to accompany
the ones he
imagined at
the Palermo Zoo,

and the Tyger
of Blake's visions,
not to forget
their rendition

on the harmonium
of Allen Ginsberg,
have eternal seats
in the Hall of Tigers,

but we must google
other entrants.
The Mexicans Lizalde
and Jorge Cantu

stroll into binoculars,
and the one I saw
at Ranthambore,
with my son,

that President Clinton
spotted later
on his India visit.
Now Bill is not

a poet but gives
ballast to arguments
that tigers should
wander always

about in gardens
or fenced off jungles,
tee-off on the links.
I think Woods will

survive also in history
like the tiger at
Ranthambore smoked
out for dignitaries

or the Honolulu cat
that began this poem
by strolling into
headlines

whose keeper
says was the most

tame of three
and did not require

tranquilizers
to coax him back
into anonymity,
or the tiger claimed

by Viridiana Estrada
from Puebla, Mexico
who, according to
Poem Hunter

(I googled while
writing this tiger)
wrote Tyger Tyger
burning bright

and received
a comment
from Colette,
not the deceased

French writer,
but a contemporary
reader, who loved
the rhythm,

"air of mystery
and questioning"
in Viridiana' s
adopted tiger.

AFTER THE PARTY

in Memoriam: Anura Bandaranaike

I remember an evening
flavored by my mother's
cooking, bringing
two smart patriots
together, to speak
about devolution
not yet realized,
accommodate
what makes sense
seeing the island
from afar, the only
way forward,

two dear friends
who met then
for the first time.
Now, one is laid
to rest, and
the other engages
readers still
to think afresh
about slow or fast
bombs, double-speak,
cynical tongues, how
to bring more than

twenty-five years
of war to an end
before all our parties
break up and families
gather, with shotgun
shells and confetti
to scatter, at weddings

held on holy ground
beside gravestones
where fathers and
brothers, mothers
and sisters are buried.

ADJUSTMENT

We walk across railroad tracks.
It's late, the moon full, waves
roaring on the other side
of coconut trees. There
aren't any goons asking

for id's. It's 1980 or some
such year before current
flapping of metal wings, birds
alloyed everywhere dropping
pellets right on our foreheads.

Aiyo, we say, how the hell,
machan, don't buggers
know how to shoot, and
these poisons flowing
in our blood.

What's become of older
weapons of war, when
knife pricked or bomb
blew off the head but
left the next man alive

to attend to his family
and the fight? Now

cancer multiplies
his cells and we should
not walk across railroad

tracks or down on the beach
off Galle Face, which
today's children know
as a high security zone,
and their older siblings

as no-man's land, lovers'
folly, but we protest
too much, surely
we can carry passports
in our bathing trunks?

SAD TREE

Sad tree makes the rhyme
easy: sepalika, arbor-tristis,
pavazhamalli, languages
name flowers fallen

by roots, in the corner plot,
on the morning of letters
sent from the island asking
for a kiss, some prick

of love to recall early
ambling across railroad tracks
to a beach unsullied
by cadavers, freak waves,

idyll that calls
like a siren to forget
me not on a bed
of white buds crying.

RIOT

When the mob
assembled
in the plaza
outside

the Law Courts,
at the Galle Fort,
1958, friends
spirited

the Assistant
Government
Agent, my future
father, out

of its hands.
Without friends,
he would not
have lived,

married; I would
not be here
to remember
this.

O CANADA

This career appears
to have expired:
no pulse felt,

thrashing stopped
when I left the previous
post, destined

to decipher the most
bizarre country I have
ever encountered,

its absence, vast
forests full of cold
and hibernating bears.

What keys
am I offered here?
Not to city

or wilderness,
left alone at night
to brood and blather

into a tumbler,
to stroke a computer
to friends in other climes

who live and ponder
with boyfriends,
kids, mothers,

and here I am
with children
far away and poems

on my face
like left over
cream

from the morning
shave.
I did not mean

to refer only
to myself.
There are other

investigators
of new immigrants
and histories

of searching
for jobs
and establishing

roots in places
like Sasketchewan
and New Hope,

London, Ontario,
names from the past,
aborigine and European;

we have to use
the old names;
how can language itself

be made new,
the slate rubbed clean
like a breath

of freezing wind
in the camp
beside the pine trees

and the new
grave dug
to bury passports

and poems
and souvenir programs
from ancient concerts,

when Canada
did not appear
in the Tarot deck,

when a war was still
to be won, and a love rooted,
in the place you were born?

LOVING THE OTHER

You've learned right
on the island, what
a training ground
twenty-five years of war
affords; now go abroad;

there are conflicts
everywhere. In Basra and
Gaza bazaars are ticking,
and you know how
to mediate and broker

civil accords, expert
in arts of making peace.
Don't worry if you merit

odd lines in newspaper stories.
Everybody knows

how Man thrives
fighting for his plot,
uprooting trees and
hewing a cabin out
that can withstand

damned boll weevils
or the twister
from climate hell,
but we do not want
to fall into vats

where cynics bucket
their daily ration
of water. Imagine
returning to watering
holes dear flaming

countrymen and women,
shutting off generators
and dismantling
the new cricket stadium
so we can sport

a good old field
again to play, and
ride ponies in Galle,
or sing about Daisy
and cowboys

on the range. I don't
remember Sinhala
or Tamil songs, but
that's another story,
and I am in the middle

of making peace
at the bazaar
in Marrakech, and
my friend dressed
in a voluminous

black cloak ticks
my bloody ear
off, yet far from
Borella Market
I find myself

in a very public place,
among eggplant,
onions, hands,
musical instruments,
clucking chickens,

and I wonder
if this raucous
meeting
will survive
as we try

to make order
and grace
while that robed
fellow taps
his cell phone,

and back
on the island,
they say, don't
worry about
our bit

of bitterness
any more,
there are plenty
of foreign
donors

building homes
for tsunami victims,
and we go
right on heaving
sorrows

about
in the usual way,
with a bottle
of arrack,
an afternoon

lay about,
twisted
in each other's
arms,
whispering

how much
we depend
on the other,
to douse our
flaming desire.

GRANNY, A CENTURY

Reminded
of the still pool,
buffaloes and flies
round the bund,
old woman
in a frock coat,
slippers, chasing
pole cats, tongue
wagging over
morning tea

and a cutlet.
Onion skin,
oils stained
and cupped
in the armchair,
where Granny sat
for a London
year, thrice
upholstered now
over 30 years—

London,
Honolulu, Rockville,
our houses
resistant to shifts
in taste, history's
rubs, Ceylon
rolling still
out of the station
at Fort. Granny
hundred now.

FATHER

Geese honked on their way
to the other side of the sky;
rain and wind teamed
up cold and befogged
the neighbourhood
the day my father died.

The day my father died
my brother sang a lullaby
to accompany him
on his journey up high,
to that territory
where my son says

he will teach poetry,
where I say poems
will fry like butter
and geyser out of the hole
in the center of space
as if from molten rock,

My son, out of entrails
of carcasses still
fleshed, from trees
ripe with vines,
conceived in death,
hammered from memory.

Here are belts and hides,
impressed, distilled,
etched on buckles
and holsters, ola-leafed
images, parchments,
poems to survive the fires.

He has left us his name—
we wear it today—
and metaphors
that curdle and whirl
through our consciousness,
each one at its own pace

in nature's slow dying,
in its corybantic profusion,
my father, you have given
us "the Saving Cup,"
and voices from the wilderness
and caught "the undertow

of sadness, which rocks
what fleeting gladness
there is today, or may once
have been." Now, that
you have seen the vision
that enlightened your face

and suffused it smiling
in the moment of death
by the altar
of the Blessed Sacrament
in this Saint Jude Church,
now you can tell us

quietly in dreams,
as we stumble
into morning
and break our bread,
that awesome secret
which led us out

of the island and
into a history where
a turn of the head

does not make salt,
and you do not expire
in gunfire, or necklaced

with a tire, where
you can make peace
with God and guide
your children,
adore your grandchildren,
love your countries—

all the countries
woken up by
your voracious reading
as boy and man—
the countries
from which all travelers return

—the day their fathers die—

laden with gifts,

—the day our fathers die—

awesome secrets

—the day our fathers die—

ambrosia, bliss

the day Rasa, the day Guy,
the day our father died.

ELEGY FOR NEELAN TIRUCHELVAM

I walked that street as a child, under the mango trees,
Smelling bushes of white flowers gathered for temples,
My tongue a sweet shop furnished by my grandmother,
Crushed with chillies in coconut fed by her servant.

I belonged to the elite columnists liked
To attack, for its insularity, its absolute divorce
From the fratricidal reality, there on the corner
Of Rosmead Place and Kynsey Road he died.

I did not know him well, he belonged to a group
Seen from afar fighting so that its fellow citizens
Enjoy a little more of their human rights, someone
Who had a solid knowledge of the recent history

Of peacemakers in other countries who thought
That one can live with dignity, without bothering
A fly, that suddenly the human world would improve
Because of the sweat of writing new and just laws.

He exploded on the corner of Rosmead and Kynsey,
Fell with all of his blood, his ambition, to the end
That waited for him, that named him with another fame,
One more of the human beings who denied

That the nightmare could touch him, as if he had
Some immunity against the barbarians, that letters
Written in laws had the power to absorb
A bullet, to convert its powder into a flower.

Mr Tiruchelvam, I'll wait for you with a bouquet
Of flowers, all the cars are bottled up, there is no exit,
The corner is the crossing point, destiny, morning.
You are fifty-five years old, rich, famous.

There are other great figures in the country, models
Throughout the world, we are not going to be sad;
We will push forward, put your name on the lintel
Of a school, the signboard of a street, in the memoirs

Published by the civil cells you founded
So that the country can have places of reflection
Far from the crossing points, the shouting
In parliament, beating in jails, melancholy

That can bury everybody until the sun rises,
Until its children rise, until the mangos ripen,
Until the crushed chillies return to the tongue.
Even if you are far away on the shore

Of an unknown land, that you write in another
Language to make of this murder an image,
A teaching, so that you can recount these streets,
Rosmead and Kynsey that observed your play,

That now have another meaning, names of a cemetery.

COUNTRY

Serve your country
wearing crisp, white cotton
and a dandy's tie.

Serve members
of the guild, assuring
poets are paid.

Serve roots: island
story, emblem now
of all islands burning,

then roaring tipsy
before dousing
in the sea.

Serve abstract
ideas: liberty, right
to assembly. Parachute

into evening's vigil,
right cause bringing
humans together:

Katrina, Mitch,
that murderous tsunami.
Serve women, mother,

girlfriend, serve
children, son, daughter.
Serve prejudices

on a big screen.
Say I will overcome
them; gathering on

the Mall recite, I
shall from "white and
black cloud free."

Serve poetry twice,
she is your particular
love. Serve arrack

and hot cadju nuts.
Serve Deep Song.
Serve prayers

in baskets, with
loaves and fish.
Serve the beggar

before knocking
on your boss's
door, shaking

his hair, bawling
on his shoulder:
my captain,

my country,
what next?
I am already

in service
and believe still
in the last three yards

or feet, or inches,
words of endearment,
my ability to love.

COME HOME

Come home,
now—not just
for kiri bath
or poll sambol,
or a salt slick
on the beach
and a tumble
in the hammock.

Come home,
now—wandering
the planet means
nothing
if you don't
return for the party
and make
your parents glad.
Come home,
now—though
the parable
does not fit.
Father died
abroad,
and Mother's
left to keep
their house
running
for another son,
and always
local allegiances,
church
up the road,
and visitors
from England
and Australia
or the island
once called Ceylon,
where branches
of the family tree
flower still
saying:
Come home,
now—for
a stringhopper
feast,
to remember

childhood
jeeps rolling
over jungle
tracks, or
the name
of some half-
forgotten
agreement
to share
all the loaves
in the basket,
before noting
how singular
the Army
has become,
bereft of
minorities,
its esprit
du corps
changed
utterly
into a
question
of loyalty
and tribal
allegiance,
the island
lost at sea,
and now
the alarm
ringing,
time
come
for my
airport taxi.

WALK BEYOND

Will posterity toss us in the stir-fry
or roast? Shall we draft wills
against unpleasant editions of
unguarded letters and muttering
over gulfs of silence, canyons, gullies?
Help me please with topography,

names of low-lying islands and
peninsulas slated to be drowned
by seas rising, earth heating up,
such chatter infesting politics
and verse, yet who will give me
the words? Mother, son, girlfriend?

I made order and it went astray.
Gathered treasures from four
continents, ferreted the other day
into a thief's duffel bag. I lost five
pounds this week walking. Am
on the bloody mend walking. I write

lots of letters to four continents
and wonder how to link
to the first colony on the moon.
Can someone tell me if certain
knowledge of five land masses,
the continents which kept

me going through Standard Four
has been overcome by the monster
wave or the thirst to be first and
clear? Google earth, google me,
cube of tofu in the fry, light
as bean curd should feel

in assessing sustainable
free life. Will you wife
me to the end? We're almost
there, and the children must fly.
We cannot guard them against
blasts of sun or stars, wave or bombs.

THERE IT IS

I think of my country,
of black men who gather
palmyra sap and

of their children wearing
machine guns and
cyanide capsules,

Tigers who have
baptized my land—
with a ferocious and

mad fame—that fed
my grandfather
with fine birds hunted

and thrown into fire
stirred with red onions
and coconut milk

at evening when burning
wood served like a lamp
to farmers—returning

from the sun that killed
and fertilized—loyal
to values taught over

centuries, of how
to be man and woman
in each caste.

Today there are women
murderers, mayors,
divorcees and poets.

There are men
together
in small rooms

in Europe and Africa
who prepare foods
of their island and

negotiate contracts
in another language
thinking in nothing

but money; there are
conferences over
round-tables

in well-known
universities, supported
by private foundations,

conversations by
satellite, and telephone,
with speakers

who discuss new
economic strategies
for my country about

to take off, and
on the other side,
always, in the depth

of a well, in a small
living room, a big
city where islanders

meet to eat
and talk, there is
a photograph

on the wall,
it could be any
old bay, with two

coconut trees
painted by
an unknown hand

until the invitee
asks them, where,
where, is that sea?

PRIDE

Such need to be affirmed,
the ways our fathers
and mothers pronounced
the words, their lilt that marks
islanders apart from Bharat,
from all that confluence
of tongues. Here English

flourished beside Sinhala
and Tamil in an experiment
in co-existence; there was
plenty of water, Mahaveli
and other rivers, not
to mention the ocean
with its feast of prawns,

crab and kingfish,
and up in the mountains
coffee and tea and
everywhere, mangoes,
jackfruit, rambutans,
passion flowers. Of course,
the Dry Zone required

a different compromise
with the watering holes,
and beyond Elephant Pass
the vellalas tilled red earth
and made bulbous onions
and chillies, and the karavas
caught their sprats.

This idyll destroyed
by war is itself a minor
fiction given the famous
battles leading to Tamil
kings ruling in Kandy,
now the seat of Buddha's
tooth and Sinhala pride.

Who shall we celebrate
next, erect a perpetual
ecosystem for the Veddas?
A replica of the Jaffna
Public Library made

in reinforced steel
then painted?

A model intertextual
class with Sangam
poems, Vedas,
Mahavamsa,
and boys and girls
handpicked from
all the communities,

a local Brown versus
Board of Education,
no more language division,
everybody reading English,
Tamil and Sinhala,
mandated by the powers
in Colombo and Kilinochchi?

PILL FOR AN ISLAND

I did not visit the Black Pussycat,
or the Fat Flounder, even Macy's
on 34th Street. I left the Back Fence
for another return. I must devote
myself to compressing the city
into a compact, multi-purpose
pill to pop on those occasions
far away on Ceylon's East Coast

where the blue-green jeweled
sea—turned nut brown, in the wake
of the tsunami—witnesses again

patrol boats and small arms fire,
lobbed grenades and thatch explosions,
rapes of social workers and hundreds
upon hundreds upon thousands
in flight from their villages.

War has returned to the hamlets,
coves and palm-fronded taverns,
and in New York those towers
of Ilium vanished, my two islands
united in the global accounting
of war and war's alarms, everybody
bruised, jaded and afraid, waiting
for the Messiah or the flames.

WHEN WIND HURLS STONES

When wind hurls stones,
picks up straw houses,

When earth rumbles,
splits, buries buildings,

When bomb sends
bus flying in Colombo Fort,

When a good man,
precise thinker, reader

of ola leaves and
digital text, gives way

—his body opened
before surgeons—

and we try
to make sense

out of nonsense,
to understand

the boil on the brain,
blocked artery,

alarming message:
"surgery did not

go well.
We must pray."

He told me
he missed an earlier

Fort explosion
by a minute.

He had just
driven through

the roundabout.
Today, another

bomb, and in
a surgeon's ward,

I don't know where,
in Singapore or

Colombo,
we ask for doctors

we can trust,
but even

trusted
are not God,

are subject to
human vanity

and uncertainty.
Perhaps there is

no human way
to cope, except

with hands flailing,
to cut all parties

down, in grief's
general cacophony,

in the general
madness

of endless war
and endless

explosions
in the Fort,

and hearts
blocked up

in millions
of bodies

on all
the continents,

and we're left
with words,

funeral orations,
memories

of the soul
freed now

who made
our lives

glad
for a time.

LOVE AND BE LOVED

for Manik

Yes, he loved women,
with abandon, and without
jealousy. He loved the plants
villagers smoked and cooked.
He enjoyed palavering
with headman and washerwomen,

and at the end of the visit
driving off to cocktails
in the capital, party whiskey—
washed, eaten with hot prawns,
on the verandah at Barefoot,
near the sea, and rumbling

of jeeps and musical stop signs
as roads are blocked against
unwanted bombers. He loved

Tamils and Sinhalese,
Burghers and Muslims.
He wore a monk's robes

to walk away from a lawsuit.
He would say, the case
was cooked. I had no chance:
whose laws determine right
and wrong? Yet he despaired
with us about the impunity

of the current set
of rogues. The old rogues
went to Oxford but forgot
their codes upon return
to the island; they knew
at least what pretence

they surrendered
to have their perks
and sit on the elephant's
back for the duration
of their terms. But
for fifty years now

some are shot before
they finish, and thus fate
turns until kingdom
come and we sit down
before the ocean
and say: send us

another murderous
wave to wash us
away; yet we realize
always there are
rich red yolks
in the nest

who will burst and fly
and seek dry land
restoring the cycle
to live and let live
until we tip the balance
again and another

guru comes
swaddling out
of his clothes to say:
love and be loved.
There is no other
rule. Love and be loved.

CALLING CAMEROON

My father mused
in a poem about
a lass from Cameroon.
I share his sweet tooth
and scramble too
to see the Lions kick
a football in their
swashbuckling way,

but French and
English, this
co-habiting,
compels me
to visit Yaounde,
to find out if a lass
from Cameroon
may serve as envoy

to the island
of my birth
which trumpets still—
one supreme path
where war makes peace—
to stop the nonsense,
with fancy footwork,
in bilingual verse.

PLANES IN THE SKY

Feet are tired
pressed into
asphalt, climbing
the campus hill,
composing

a sparer line:
effervescence
in mist, swirling
about stones,
a girl, freckled,

jeaned,
auburn-haired
like the leaves,
walks past
my shadow,

a shadow, wish
to dissolve into
scenery, flowering

bush, wind,
chameleon

silent
on a branch
not hurt or
harassed
by predators

swooping down
from clouds:
over the A-9
Highway,
by Elephant Pass.

II. War

ABLUTION

Hungry, tired,
on my stomach
in a bunker,
counting time,
I climb out

eventually,
to relieve
myself, boil
water for tea,
dry food

remains
in the bunker,
my children
bunkered, I hear
whistling,

I whistle,
swirl, roar,
pick shrapnel
out with
my fingers.

ONE OF US

During civilized periods
in the history of kingdoms,
courtiers, or the king's
person himself,
in audience

with the gadfly,
would offer the fellow
death or exile.

These days
assassins
butcher their fly
in daylight
near security
checkpoints
in front of
bewildered subjects.

My Lord,
Dutugemunu,
slayer of wild beasts
in northern
jungles, why must
we kill brother
Lasantha, shed
our own blood?

TO THE COURTS, IN REMORSE

Drop all charges against
the scribe, Tissanaiyagam.
His glaucoma needs
treatment and his wife
will be grateful,

. . . and the Dean of
the Diplomatic Corps
will feel less inclined

to speak at public
acts of grievance—

Ok, I agree we must not
interfere with funerals,
leaves a bitter taste
on the BBC's tongue.
Inevitably, our advisors

will counsel banning
that Commonwealth
voice. But then we must
cope with reporters
in disguise, especially

these pesky bloggers
who feel empowered
to write what they see
and hear, taste and
touch, as if witness

can make bread out
of flour, or yams
sprout, in a mineswept
Vanni. And let me
not forget

the political analysts
who worry in public
that a failed state
will be our cup of tea.
I trust you will still drink

our fabled single leaf
beverage and visit
our white sand,
black sand, red sand,
blue sand beaches.

DANCING IN SYMPATHY
(MULLAITIVU)

Six boys
from Hindu College
will enter the scene
Stage Left,

an equal
number of girls
from Muslim Ladies
Stage Right.

They will shake
their bodies,
slide and writhe,
and be still

to rid bones
of chains
and memories,
and invite

guests, us,
to sway
in harmony
even if

we're away
from jungles
which give
shelter, or

ash-filled
homes
whose roofs
are open

to whistling
bombs
and winds
that sweep

left-overs
clean. That
Boxing Day
the tsunami

swept
residents
out; now
the Army

marches in
four years
later to find
an abandoned

town, and
in nearby
woods
yakshas

howling
in Tamil
calling
for food

and water,
medicine,
safe passage
south . . .

while in
the capital,

as I imagine
the performance

must end,
on a stage
a boy and girl
will embrace.

MEMO
(ABOUT ORDNANCE)

The biodegradable bomb
causes no collateral
damage if left
unexploded
in a field
when the war ends.

Raindrops
will strike the
material into
effervescence
and farmers can
till again assured.

In this age
of restoring science—
flying cars and
sequestering carbon
at a healthy clip—
we should devote

resources
to the unpleasant

but necessary task
of assuring our weapons
supply, that it keeps
to current ethical

standards, that future
killing by the State
will be precise, targeted,
not tied to elections
in this country or abroad,
and biodegradable.

JUNGLE,
MULLAITIVU

250,000
civilians,
non-combatants,
wielders
of pitchforks,
carrying clothes
on their backs,

pots,
photographs,
huddled
under giant
jungle trees
watching
for serpents

by cross-fire
caught,

trapped in
blast light,
snapped
shut,
shut

snapped,
hidden,
exposed,
cadavered,
while I eat
and sleep
and write.

EQUAL TREATMENT

Citizens
of Kilinochchi
and Mullaitivu
fled before
our liberators
arrived.

They live
for the moment
in nearby jungle
under a canopy
punctured
by shells.

Some moved
to a safe zone
demarcated
by liberators

where they
have fallen

since to errant fire.
Others ran into
liberators' arms
and live now
protected in large
barb-wired camps.

FORGETTING, MULLAITIVU

The town is full of stray
dogs, cows, ghosts,
buildings pockmarked,

unhinged, open to wind
and rain. Soldiers patrol
on foot. Trucks and tanks

rumble through the center.
Rebels took all the fittings
to jungle cellars, and we wait

eagerly to discover how
the Supreme Leader makes
his bed. Look at Europe today,

Germany lost five hundred kilometers
on its eastern flank. How many
young people know this history?

We will disappear. The tsunami
swept a lot away. Our failing
memory compensates for the rest.

EMPATHY
(ACROSS THE PALK STRAIT)

Fifty-six million Tamils
in South India share
lower body parts and
brains with brothers
and sisters in the Vanni.

They also share
essential fears
and dreams as well
as bodily functions
with the rest of

the human race. So
I would be grateful
if the journalist seeking
to close his story
on the special relationship

of India to the conflict
would leave it unfinished,
unexplained, open
to contradiction by uneducated
yet sympathetic readers

from places beyond India,
humanists, who see themselves
in civilian clothes, huddled
under trees, running away
from shells, trying to escape death.

THE BIG EYE

When Orwell wrote that war is peace
literature may have solved hypocrisy
once and for all, and new generations

of politicians learned his lesson
in their graduate programs, or on the job,
paying heed as a result to eyewitness

accounts of atrocities committed
by the good army liberating
the Vanni from Tiger devils.

The fact that the same eyewitnesses
speak of convoys of wounded
and dying blocked by the devils

gives their accounts an appearance
of impartiality, seriousness,
but as the man in charge

in the capital said, there are only
four of these international observers
and the rest are locals and all

are subject to Tiger pressure.
Locals certainly cannot be trusted.
They speak Tamil and live

in harmony with cousins
in Chennai and are suspicious
of detention camps where

we welcome entire families
to eat and live, watched,
protected, in peace.

DISCO, COLOMBO

Boogie woogie baby,
ease your bum
out of its slum
and shake shake,
celebrate;

news from the
front is sweet;
I just read
the ministry's
website,

even foreign
correspondents
report the Tigers
are trapped
in a sandwich.

This war will end
and all the zealots
in Tamil Nadu
can fly their kites.
We are united,

the lion is roaring
wind on the flagpost
over the bakery.
His loaves are fresh,
our lovemaking

sweeter, and
we can eat
kolikutu plantains
in peace, visit
the Temple

of the Tooth
and swim
at Unawatuna,
play and prayer
that kept us sane

in days before
war and tsunami,
and I see
the market
is bullish

on cement today
now that we can
rebuild the plant
at Kankesanturai
which sits

on limestone,
to produce
headstones too
for the unfortunate
civilian dead.

BOMB PICKING

My friend says
that where ashes
fall from the grill
nothing grows,
not even weeds,
for a year. Imagine

recovering land
from artillery
shells, cluster
bombs shattered
and multiplied,
the sheer slow

picking up
of signals
with metal rods,
mistakes,
explosions.
I heard today

that removing
the world's
unexploded bombs
would take
five or six or ten
thousand years,

I don't have
the exact number
—an elusive target—
don't know how
many more devices
will drop in 2009.

THE THING ITSELF

Muthukumaran
visits me,
his solitary
protest

outside
the central
government
office

in Chennai,
dousing
himself
in kerosene

and burning
until rescue,
though chances
of survival

are bleak.
He wanted
attention
paid

he said
to burning
issue of Tamils
in Sri Lanka.

Muthukumaran,
a poet,
burning
his metaphor.

THE TWAIN SHALL MEET

This Independence Day
let us gaze with
renewed vigor
at our northern forests
resplendent in the light
of flares and
potassium nitrate.
The savvy beasts
who wandered
there and knew
the earth had shifted
astray, the tsunami

would strike,
have yet to develop
a sixth sense
for human bombs,
even after twenty-five years
of war, and deserve

to be saved;
as for their guests
from the towns
of Kilinochchi
and Mullaitivu,
Elephant Pass,

let's clear jungle paths
for the International
Committee of the Red
Cross and our flag-bearing
soldier boys from the South.

TIGER SHIRT

When soldiers
discovered
the tiled and
air-conditioned
two-storey bunker
hidden in a coconut
plantation, they

also found a size
42 dress shirt
from Marks & Spencer;
but reports don't say
if any of our boys
tried Prabhakaran's
shirt for size.

CRICKET AND WAR

There is no justice in getting
hammered on our own turf; Indian
cricketers wound our pride though
our boys have won all but one hundred
square miles of the North. Civilians

living with Tigers have been given
forty-eight hours to walk through jungle,
stepping past land mines and
snakes dragging wounded
to PDK hospital outside

the Safe Zone we demarcated
to offer them refuge. No hospitals
can operate in rebel territory,
our minister explained
to Sky TV, simply not cricket

to question sovereign interpretation
of rules of war about safe
passage for sick and wounded
to an unauthorized medical plant
where shells might finish them off.

APPEAL

Puthukudiyiruppu Hospital   *For Immediate Release*

Do not bomb
our pediatric unit.

Do not bomb
our women's ward.

Do not bomb
patients sleeping

on mats between
beds or patients

lying on the beds.
Do not bomb

injured brought
on pickup trucks,

draped on tractors,
hobbling on foot,

astride bicycles.
Do not bomb

and henceforth
beware

humanitarian law.
Beware Interpol.

Beware foreign trips.
Beware membership

in regional and
international

organizations.
Beware errant

lawyers, mothers,
beware ghosts.

BY OTHER MEANS

This war will end
in days,
government says,

before I finish
my poetry book,
and the thirteenth or

some other
amendment's
imposed

in the now
shell-shocked
northeast, and

Devananda
ride an
armored carrier

up the A-9,
on Jaffna
High Street,

as Lasantha
predicted,
and Chennai

cousins fustigate
their central
government

for applying
principle
of non-intervention

except
in cricket,
and dancing

bells clang
decibels
through

the capital,
and this
writing

pursue peace
by other
means,

such as
discreet,
measured, silence.

TO EACH HIS OWN

This German pope, along
with his ambassador
in Colombo, Dean of the
Diplomatic Corps,

should respect
our island sovereignty.
We know how to clean
house. Diplomats

should shut up and
religious leaders return
to their original briefs:
candidates in different

stages of beatification
need papal review.
I understand a cry
for help at times

of ecological disaster—
when the tsunami

pummelled us
for example—but today

on this sixty-first anniversary
of our independence,
we do not need guidance,
or public cries of conscience.

QUESTION OF ARMS SALES

Arms manufacturers
of the world, unite,
and bring your top
sales force together
for emergency talks.

Government says
the war will end.
Will it decommission
troops? Reduce
the weapons budget?

These are alarming,
though unlikely,
outcomes. Yet,
we must prepare.
Who knows?

Tigers may
regroup in Malaysia,
or found sleeper
cells in Nagakoil.
Government

must understand,
its navy can
never stop
patrolling
the seas.

War on Terror,
once declared,
is permanent,
impossible
conceptually

to remove
from psyche
and language.
So arms dealers
of the world,

I conclude,
don't worry,
you can still
sell to Sri Lanka
and create

new markets
as well,
in Madurai,
Chennai,
Land's End.

JUST IN TIME

History is told by the victors
except in Sri Lanka. There
are too many cooks
bothering with our curry

and Tigers, once
deadly with gun and bomb,
have turned now
to propaganda to achieve

their eelam, shaping
the language of aid groups
and western liberal
democracies. I am sorry

that even the war
on terror will no longer
form part of the lexicon.
Am glad we acted

in time while
the pussycats slept
and Americans
conducted their primaries.

SURVEYOR'S PLANS (FEARS)

The Vanni
is pockmarked
by villagers and
plots where yams

and onions
are grown. There
are cows, of course,
and chickens, and
Tamils spread
about the property.

Now, this war
is driving people
off their land. Slowly
we are seeing
refashioning of
land use, less
seeds cultivated,
more fields
left fallow—
booby-trapped

by heartless cats
who have kept
villagers hostage
for all these years.
We must not
let the parcels go
to waste. We
must create
new deeds,
review

at least
Government
Agent records.
rebuild and
repopulate
Sri Lankan earth
with Sri Lankans,
genuine,
peace-loving
multi-ethnic.

LANGUAGE ISSUE

We, Sri Lankans, delight
in spinning English
words into local linguistic
tapestries, especially
in the department
of community relations.

Racism is impossible
in our chauvinist
lexicon, ethnic cleansing
becomes a communal
riot. Bodies are burnt,
washed up on beaches,

nevertheless, this crude
reckoning happens
on the margins
of discourse, outside
parliament, courts,
and the president's

residence at Temple Trees,
up the A-9, in the wildlands
of the Vanni. Now naysayers
remember bombs
in the Pettah, on Flower Road,
in Colombo.

By equal proportion
is their phrase, tit for tat,
state versus terrorists,
forgetting the backdrop,
farmers and their families,
bloody victims and audience.

MURDER INVESTIGATION: INTERVIEW

Who is Lasantha?
What is Lasantha?
Why one murder
among so many
on the planet?

He wrote to a tabloid,
attacked every
president and
prime minister.
So many suffered him.

As for me, I took
him to courts.
Isn't that the right
approach, to sue
the scribe?

Now, let's move
on to current
matters, either
you are with us
or the terrorists, BBC.

OUR STORY

The brigadier speaks
of the other side's long reach,
the way it herds terrified
civilians back into harm's way

from refuge in the Safe Zone
where shells fall but only
from the other side, where
if the State fires it is

because terrorists set up
guns beside civilians.
Given fifty thousand troops
liberating Vanni, I wonder

why goverment cannot
cordon off the Safe Zone,
really secure it for civilians,
so it cannot be subject

to shooting, requiring
response in press
conferences, on websites,
so international hounds

will stop yapping
and accept government methods
of sniffing out game,
clearing land for new planting.

FIRE DEPARTMENT

Where is your village?
Burning.

Where is your village?
Mined fields.

Where is your village?
Blasted in crossfire,

wounded under
jungle trees.

Where is your village?
Running across

marshes, shot
in the back.

Where is your village?
Waving white flags

frisked, registered,
supervised in a camp.

Where is your village?
Blowing up army

friskers,
other villagers.

Where is your village?
Toronto, Berlin,

Tamil Nadu.
Where is your village?

Madagascar as option
has not been discussed.

Where is your village?

Hasta la vista,
Special Envoy!

Where is your village?
Burning.

APPENDICITIS

Inscribing
names of dead
on a memorial wall
gives no pleasure.

Turning
from the notebook
I glance outside
the window

to snow-capped peaks
far from Sri Lanka,
yet as the planet
will know soon

Russian and
American satellites
crashed last night,
adding tons of debris,

hurtling faster
than bullets,
to the Milky Way,
a fresh field of worry

for the human race
as it prepares
its journey
to a new ecosystem

where butchery
of neighbors
will not define
relations,

will just be
a distant memory
from Old Europe,
an appendix.

HARVEST

Brothers and sisters
shelled, shot, bombed
while elsewhere

on the globe,
dancers celebrate
the harvest,

men stamp feet
in toned leather shoes,
women like butterflies

swirling soft-soled,
and I, on a swing,
a yo-yo, before

beating feet
on stage. I should
have entered

a monastery,
shut down internet,
prayed for an

inter-galactic explosion,
the shape of a pearl,
beauty of a thousand

gunships flying
over a flaming
forest ball,

Saturday night
Sri Lanka
suicide, dance hall.

ANOTHER COUNTRY

We dance
in the square
among friends.

The trova is strong,
wind refreshing,
we are at peace.

A bomb does not
wait for us
at the corner,

or a kidnapper
stare, seeking
his chance

to spirit us
away from
the dance floor.

We do not live
in Sri Lanka.
We do not enjoy

a state of
emergency.
We are like

anybody else,
hopeful we will
wake up tomorrow.

SMOKE SIGNAL

The sense
of a life,
dousing body
in gasoline,
ablaze
before Lake
Geneva,
brought back
to London
for burial,

sacrifice
conducted
in exile,
a funeral,
valued

news item,
drawing
attention
to burning
of family

in Vanni
while
numbed,
comatose,
Tamils
wake up
abroad
to light
stoves
to make

coffee
and read
about
their pyre
burning
crisply
in Swiss
air
outside
UNHCR.

VICTORY AND DEFEAT

Let us throw these words,
victory and defeat,
into the dustbin.

Mastering illusion
is the only way out
of the maze. Learn

the art of mapmaking.
Find your own way
out of hell.

Use gods and
preachers. Use
poetry.

But do not listen
to rants of those
who say victory

is close at hand,
around the corner,
one bomb away.

SCULPTURE: IN MEMORIAM

I have not learned
how to use a gun;
thought I could live
out the line in my hand
without recourse
to suicide or murder,

which would hurt
family and friends,
and leave unsettling
questions for the literary
executor: how to classify
making verses beyond

the border, unhinged,
crossing over with
Meinhof, or Reznikoff
deciding to stop
writing for five years,
though Socrates kept

mind limber acquiring
a new language
in the days before
he took hemlock,
but contradictions
visit once more, near

my home in Vancouver,
a poet named Stuart,
once the great hope
of the city, now resigned
to an SRO on the East Side,
as I gather shrapnel up

from various news reports
to make a sculpture
to send to an imaginary
museum to be built
on the land bridge
between Tamil Nadu

and Talaimannar,
the one where
Hanuman's monkey
army formed a chain
Rama rode over
to rescue his Sita.

What a silly story!
Sita lives

in Toronto now
and Rama burned
himself to death
in Geneva.

OVERHEARD IN THE CAPITAL

Varatharaja's tongue has loosened
again. He told the BBC
that fifteen civilians were killed
and one hundred wounded over the last
two days, and shells were raining
on the Safe Zone and outside.

Now I understand he is our man,
sent by the General Medical Officer,
but he has become deranged,
hostage to the LTTE,
his reports are not credible,
positively incredible, to suggest

there is a severe shortage
of food, and no medicines
for surgery, and what is
this hospital he has made
in the jungle hanging
IVs on branches.

We must remove his telephone,
get him out for his own safety,
rehabilitated in one of the camps.
We do not need Kurtz
howling in the heart
of the Vanni.

HEALING (UNFINISHED)

Varatharaja is doctor in the Vanni.
When my grandfather served
as GMO Jaffna, when he
toured the country
as District Medical Officer,
he brought stethoscope
and aspirin to villages
in the jungle.

He told me about the fight
between cobra and mongoose,
how cobra bit mongoose
before having head torn
off and mongoose scampering
to a bush to wipe his wound
with the medicinal leaf,
to survive, to fight again.

My grandfather would
have been shocked and
saddened by these shells
and mortars, this constant
whistling, five tons of metal
showered every day on the Vanni,
but he would have made his rounds,
doctors will heal, for their oath

and nature, and he must
have known about the Great War
and fighting in trenches
from studies in England.
He would have made sense
of circumstances, carried
on stubbornly to bring unguents
to the distraught, healing

with his hands, making
tourniquets from shirts
stripped off throbbing,
wounded bodies, worked
like Varatharaja,today,
in most trying conditions,
bringing a good name
to healing, giving heart

to relatives far away whose hopes
depend on his hands,
his ingenuity. Dr Varatharaja,
Dr G A Amirthanayagam salutes
you here through his grandson,
your servant and scribe,
may you live long,
may you thrive.

UNSOLICITED ADVICE

While the bureaucrat fulminates
about the cost of hotel rooms
in Geneva and the great burden
placed on the Sri Lankan government
to have to pay exorbitant rates,

he may wish to report back
to Colombo, that the most efficient
way to avoid such soaring costs
is to conduct a human rights policy
that shows some affection for the starving,

shot up, and terrified civilians—
all 70,200 or 300,000 of them—
caught at the moment in their ancestral
lands in the Vanni, burrowing into
bunkers, dying when they come out.

EXPATRIATE

Use a wide angle lens
to bomb. Do not
be stingy, embrace
the land as if
it embraced you.
There is beauty

in the line
"it is finished,"
this mortal coil,
our damned
nature redeemed.
Let us be sure

to allow them
churches, and jobs
again as clerks.
Let cousins
abroad send visas
and tickets.

We shall remain
a net exporter
of small nations,
and we shall
have peace
at home for a time.

IMPORTANCE OF BATCH MATES

Discussing house searches
on the internet or by telephone
leads to more house
inquiries. A conversation

in a public garden offers
an alternative as long
as you are not followed
into the rose bushes . . .

Perhaps a trip to a beach
hotel at Unawatuna may
lend the appearance
of a carefree holiday

and you can sit down
there with friends
and talk about police
and army, how the former

can benefit from training,
that searches should
not be a pretext for
fondling a woman's

body with an eye, or
demanding a bribe,
that army boys at least
keep their distance.

But how many
house calls take place,
and in which
neighborhoods, no one

dares to venture
a number, just that
they form part of
the atmosphere

like imminent rain
or a sunshower,
or the visit
of a white van

swift and silent
in removing prey,
nobody hearing
any scuffle, and

the erstwhile editor
who typed copy
with scorn and sadness
packs his bags and

prepares to leave
for the airport
accompanied by
a friend in the police,

someone with whom
he studied in school,
a batch mate, loyal,
able still to save his life.

OBSERVATION

This is no sport,
we are not talking
photo finish, or
innings victory.

These are humans,
card–carrying
citizens of our
socialist republic.

In the spot lights,
the white flash
of bombs,
they are dying.

SYMPATHY

Besieged on all sides,
I have sea and death
on all sides. I don't have
water to drink, just salt slicks,
not rice or dhal, nothing,
bombs and bullets, I am
unhappy, my son killed,
and you watching me
with sympathetic stares,

a black body in a loin cloth,
whites of eyes swinging
about my head, and I hear

wailing from other beds
and see doctors trying
to heal oozing wounds
and now earth blasted
a huge hole, a chance
to run, to what afterlife?

How long will I need
to regain my calm
when cousins abroad
say even modern
life in the West
offers only guilty
cups of tea and
unbearable sympathy
from neighbors?

WOMAN: MENIK CAMP

I have not visited the camp,
I cannot bear witness
to the woman who holds
her urine and feces
until nightfall before
disappearing near
the perimeter fence,
in snake-ridden grass,
under the overseer's moon,
to relieve herself.

I can tell you, the rewrite
man is useful, highlights
the story's essence,

woman's bladder full,
refusing water by 3
or 4 PM, in a sort
of Anti-Tea, hungry
and thirsty, waiting
for the absence of light,
the consolation of night.

COUP DE GRACE

Split the word, mul li vaay kkal,
name on a map called No Fire Zone,
photos of corpses, abandoned
wheelchair, couple clasped

together dead, a few vershti-d
men walking past rubble,
e-mail, news of a doctor killed,
three nurses, sixty-four patients, family

members, passersby: instant
denial by government
and its favourite line:
this was a suicide attack

(against the only
operating hospital
in the spit of beach
called Eelam.)

BBC, however, reports
the story, New York
Times gives prominence
to government spokesmen

but allows readers access
to Tamilnet website and
the pictures. A bloody
balance. Government

in a dither, cannot
stop foreign papers
from citing Tiger
propaganda.

Who are the Tigers,
now, a passerby
asked out loud
at a protest rally?

OLD TAMIL, NEW TAMIL

"We are all Tigers today
and Tamils," he told me.

"Your words about
political space to decide
who will receive new lights
or even a classroom
are not credible before
daily round-ups of people,

night shootings in Batti
and Trinco, the general
malaise about the next stop
on the route ploughed by
the white van through
our neighborhoods.

We know you have
begrudged us a province
or two, split, afraid
that together we might
cause mischief again.
Not to worry.

We are all Tigers today
and Tamils.

You may think
we shall sleep
at night later on
muttering nama
shri lanka
under patriotic

moustaches,
to our children
by their oil lamps,
such lights noted
in satellite images
beside the craters.

We are Tigers today
and Tamils.

Our boys and girls
have died. Our non-
combatants,
old people and
children have died.
The rest of us hop

on one foot but
we can still tell
a few stories

and we will vote again
when you are not
paying attention,

observed by
election monitors,
who don't speak
Chinese or Russian,
who care only to count
our votes so the ponniahs

may be driven back
to Colombo,
on their armored
carriers, and we can place
our trust in a new slate
that will lead us to Eelam."

SATELLITE VIEW

There will be lamentations
and regrets, there are already,
and recriminations. Why
did we allow the unthinkable
to fall down on those
hapless families
in tents and bunkers?

Why did we agree
only to informal
meetings
in the basement
of UN headquarters

before proposing
an emergency session

of the Human Rights
Council for next week?
After months of
slaughter, next week?
How long do we need
to assemble diplomats
of forty-seven countries

who live in greater
Geneva, some just
a walk away
from the roundtable?
I imagine the table
round like the large
hearts of hapless

bystander diplomats
before the rain
of terror, bombs
and mortar, metallic
lassos thrown
about Tamils
squared

in 2.5 kilometers
between lagoon
and sea, 50,000
civilians left
in that spit of Vanni,
numbers reduced by
tens and hundreds

every day. You ask
about other options,
such as India, or

stiffening terms
of the IMF loan,
an armed force
to separate the parties?

Yes, dear Romans,
we can choose to censure
miscreants. When a man
or state or rebel group
kills wantonly
we must stop him
or it, walk into

the line of sight,
settle the matter
with our most
special forces.
Who is right—
government
controlled by zealots,

who believe
the island belongs
first to Sinhalese
while other
residents are subject
to extra-judicial
measures

such as roundups
in unmarked vans
and denouncing
for bizarre
collaborations
with terrorist
fighter jets--

or the aforementioned
liberation fighters?

Or do we have
the last word,
survivors of
streets of Geneva
or New York

or Beijing, suited
and stuffed
with ideals
or pragmatic like
moneylenders
weighing assets
of the nation

come to pawn
its Tamil jewels
in return for
a naval base,
a wedge around
India, uninterrupted
supply of fighter

jets and expert
advice in the art
of war, in the age
of CNN, where
the first principle
denies journalists
the chance to speak

with survivors
of the slaughter
which could have
been prevented
if prying eyes
along with
aid workers
from abroad

had been allowed
inside the Vanni
to accompany
local and expendable
employees,
Tamil speakers,

subject to pressure
from Tiger overlords,
whose pictures
of injured and dead
are stage sets,
according to
government,

whose reports
to BBC are spoken
while a Tiger
points a gun
at the telephone.
Come, come,
ye spokespersons,

do you take us
for imbeciles walking
into roundtables
in Western capitals
or even in Beijing?
When food, water,
medicine, and soft

drinks are scarce
in the theater
of war, can supplies
of stage blood
be made available
like rain and heat,
mortar and missiles?

TO THE GOVERNMENT

You have killed our Man. You must
be thrilled, cult of death, black tigers,
cyanide, claymore mines blasted away,
shelled, cluster-bombed into memory,
and now picking easy in camps,

young women held away from
young men, fathers and mothers
wandering away from children, bruised
bones, shrapnel lodged in various parts
of the host: heart, face, buttocks,

and eyes rolling, miserable, waiting
for death in open-air cots outside
makeshift treatment centers
while paramilitaries hunt behind
barbed wire, mopping up

while we seethe abroad, hearing
public, soul-crunching laments,
of how we must sift within
our communities, take a hard look
at support for ravenous, murderous

beasts, and yet turning blind
from such concentrated light I don't
see why victims of more than
fifty years of state-conceived violence
must be the first to apologize.

III. After

THE NEW ARK

Two of each
species. Slugs,
orchids—wind
carried the seeds—

butterflies, Kandyan
elephants, joined
the Sinhalese aboard
Sri Lanka's ark,

its banner unfurled,
roaring, despite
inclement weather
winds howling ·

yakshas outside,
souls clamoring
for rest, lamentations
of exiled Tamils.

BELONGING

The island belongs
to centipede,
rat, butterfly,
lots of species
each with
their own habitats,
and supervising
all arable and

fallow land
the president king.

Minorities
may enjoy
clean living
in freshly cleared
forest patches,
welfare villages
with amenities
such as latrines
and tents,
gated communities.

AFTER BATTLE

Call me a fool to bow before Myth,
rotund, middle-aged, framed with cubs,
to believe in rights derived from soil
and birth, to think my voice will be heard

while guns blast away. There is one truth
I would like to share. The dictator knows
it more than fellow residents on earth,
listening to pounding on the door

from a faithful aide-de-camp
who says Swiss bankers are releasing
names of deposit holders,
a single engine plane

rumbles outside the window,
come away, Man, run
with your pockets filled
and hands free, with your wife

and children, pockets filled
and hands free, your speech
tucked in the inside sleeve
delivered at Oxford in glad

and misguided youth that said,
when pressed against the sea wall,
blindfolded, punched in the stomach
left to wait for a bullet,

especially then, show compassion,
love your enemy, pirouette,
mix your blood with the earth,
become a stain in the heart,

a voice in sleep, a memory
that insists on rising with the sun,
in the crying of fowl, growl
of an armored convoy

like thunder and rain
until the monsoon returns
to the sea and babies' milk
curdles again left out

in this unforgiving heat,
tickling ant song,
peace beyond
understanding

of craters and graves,
hulks of schoolbuses,
spit of sand between
lagoon and sea.

SRI LANKA SNAPSHOT, 2010

for residents and visitors

The leafy giant mango
tree in the back garden
has been cut down
screamed the poet,

Scar and the hyenas
are in charge, the stomach
queasy, revolted,
Il Duce megaphoned

War is Peace;
in the exhaust fumes
of a white van a soul
flits about then vanishes,

betrayal on four million
tongues, the State is Me
yet some of me is afraid
to return, to stay, paralysed

while State police black shirts
twirling clubs pulp Lasantha
to welcome in the year
that ends with Sarath abducted,

the State afraid will cover
all tracks, Defense is
Offense, Minister draws
sap at Duttu's right hand,

while his boys play cricket
for the nation and liberals
cower before the impressive
exertion of force and law

to suppress dissent, under
the ever-present pings
of execution on camera phone,
cerebral matter splattered

to disco beats, while
new-born howls alleviate
the gloom, breathing air
in the bloody morning room.

ODE TO THE HAIR

I thought of resigning. What's the point
of continuing to cultivate foreign earth?
In the end one has to buy a rifle
and return to the island where if death
pounces on you suddenly it would

only feed the god of lost causes,
and one more poet nourished
in the West shouting freedom
for the writer will be a laughing post
in the island's press dominated

by the Moustache. The former leader
of the Tigers displayed facial hair
as well, signifies manliness, bravery,
sacrifice. The general who beat him
would brush his fuzz before the mirror,

and I wanted to land in the country's heart
on its most sought-after intestinal helipads
to leave a poetry book worthy of a life dedicated
to contemplating the profound roots of follicles,
the island's underbelly buried in a hair.

OUTSIDE OF JAFFNA

I need your support, a bedside table
to place this book; my parents
and their culture gave me the gift
of speech and everywhere I stick out
my tongue with its fragile muscles.

Have you ever eaten tongue,
from the cow or some other
mammal that forms part
of our heritage? I have gotten
off easy from the dining table

thanks to my cautious approach
before the hunger of dinner guests,
ministers and their settling
of accounts. I do not travel to Jaffna,
what I used to call the North Pole

of my consciousness
that turns now on its own orbit,
a lost world where visitors
from abroad receive poison
in their food, the fashion

in that traditional city
of eliminating one's enemy.
I don't know why I need
to tell you this fact
of the city after war,

the scab of the old injury
remains still, which I like
to scratch in poems,
in your lap. Friend,
help me find some rest.

NOCTURNE

I read the island's news amused
and horrified: power grabs, riding
rough-shod over beggars, riotous
cock crowing king of his harem,

the way bodies ebb and disappear
into sea washed up later in dreams,
easy terror dispatching a white van
once to a friend's home and office,

enough to silence him
without a silencer or beat
his brain with a hammer.
I could avoid more gruesome

treatments, poetry should
be subtle, devious in purpose,
but my former island home
does not pretend to ingenuity:

thugs and vandals, mock
trials, court-martials, rule
by emergency decree,
changing traffic patterns

when the Big Man
of government and his ministers
step out to visit girlfriends,
subjects, drinking buddies.

SHORE CLEANUP

In 1972, Sri Lanka's
new government,
fresh from the baptismal
font, signed the Flora
and Fauna Act, basis
for more than thirty-eight years

of conserving the nation's
diverse species, including
five of the world's
seven seafaring turtles,
which choose the island's
beaches to nest, and thanks

to the law and decades
of villager, city-folk and
tourist education, continue
to return to shore despite
impediments in the water,
bleached, soggy bodies

of diverse and diminishing
minorities washing up
like logs, seeping into foreign
analyses of rights and freedoms,
reminders of separate and
unequal clearing of wilderness.

RENUNCIATION

We turned out of bed
saddened and furious
when we heard
Taliban detonated
the Bamiyan Buddhas:

What savagery,
to destroy testaments,
aged over centuries,
to a now effaced history.
But let us rejoice today,

Akon the singer
has been denied
a visa and a chance
to feed unruly and
sexual minds

of a sold-out
Sri Lankan crowd,
Christians no doubt,
urbane Muslims
certainly, even some

fallen gautamas,
they can't be trusted
pogo dancing,
and we don't want
skin exposed

near Lord Buddha.
Yet, I wish to offer
a disclaimer
along with a refusal
to appear before

a court-martial
or an investigative judge
to testify the nature
of We
to which I belong.

TWO LAGOONS

The history I bring
to the dinner table
stretches its neck
to feed on algae
in Kokkilai Lagoon.

It will accompany
me always describing
an obsolete idyll,
a daily lifestyle
already in the past.

Now another lagoon
appears, Nandikadal,
burial ground
for men and Tigers,
impossible dreams.

How can we heal
its waters, offer
food, light candles,
try our best
to pacify those

restless spirits
that ask us,
who walk still
on earth, how
will we overcome

the ancient
curse? Spilling
blood requires
another sacrifice,
another bloodbath.

PARENTAL ADVISORY

I do not feel joy or
pleasure, hearing
these poems
about savagery
on the island

will be published,
that my editor and
friends want
to read the new
manuscript,

our mutual desire
for catharsis could
bother a customs
inspector
at the airport;

we must take care
not to carry

back any copies,
this perennial
Tamil caution,

old style,
Satyagraha
and bills before
parliament, where
it used to stand

facing Galle Face
Green, its new purpose
the Presidential
Secretariat;
there is useful irony

in contemporary
assumption
of executive power
and legislative
weakness, I wonder

if this poem is simple,
that it should dissemble
 with more elaborate
metaphors. I have
other worries, now,

my son and
daughter,
they require time,
not poetry,
or island thuggery.

THIS BODY

Fornicate wisely, and across
a variety of academic
departments. On the run,
at conferences, invited
strategically to high schools,

once a year, expert
in husbandry of early writers,
hands well off young Virginias
and Isidoras, dancing
for the visiting dignitary,

but no such rule
for their teachers
who serve as chaperones
to festive meals and
plan conversations

about dark impulses
behind the darkness striking
that spit of beach
with fine Chinese bombs,
your poems stripped bare

by spinsters, even,
walking late at night
dreaming after wine
of being young and able
and immortal, that sex

confirms love, that
due care avoids
unfortunate rearing
after the ninth month
midnight, and death,

a cipher, a figure
in some romantic poem,
be not proud, here
we shall make peace
and drive the devils

back to their hangars.
Sylvia gave me the means,
the beat. I was sixteen
and believed, still do,
that the inchoate dilemmas

and raging contradictions
of uncivil war, trammelled
politics, and expulsion
of innocents, will find solace,
a home, hammered out in verse.

This is my verse,
muttered daily
under my breath,
spoken at night, to Moon,
to girlfriend, across

all the departments.
Hear me now. This war
will find recompense;
there shall be
no forgetting

even if government
linguists and
archaeologists
obliterate inconvenient
truths about early

settlements,
this memory's beaten
out in verse, as in the old
epics, danced and clapped,
spilt blood made flesh.

As the boy says,
who lost father and
mother, we have
to move on.
We must learn a trade.

THE THIRTY-YEAR-OLD BOY

I would like to believe
we have been forgiven,
that the end justifies

means, that prejudice
has been copy-edited out
of the nursery reader,

that the black man
with roving eyes
and moneyed breath

is not after all Tamil,
a dirty devil come
to spook our children

at night who wish only
to dream of sweets
and cricket, and how

they pumped
the minority during
tea-break in front

of the tuck shop
in a public hazing,
not approved

but allowed
by benign authority,
the Principal

of laissez-faire—
oh let our boys
steam off,

better now
than grown up
angry with wives

or trying to get jobs
in Tamil-run Public
Works Department,

or the Civil Service,
or even the thosai kaddai.
Of course that is history

now, the Thirty Year
War has been won,
and Tamil shopkeepers

must hide
their newspapers
under lungis,

and speak Sinhala
at checkpoints,
or while seeking

entry into
government buildings.
Their identity cards

will betray them
constantly of course,
as we noted

in Afrikaan guidance
read in preparing
our civic practice,

administration
of our post-1956
democracy based

on tyranny
of the majority
and the humble

subservience
of these once
mighty clerks.

Let them eat
strings. Let them
learn that when

one party wins,
another gets
kicked in the butt,

that pottus are
walking invitations
to unseemly violations,

that 100,000
relations are still
under lock and key

in Northern camps,
that cleaning up
must be sped up

so we can get these
potential voters
out to their farms

and shacks so
they can prepare
succulent meals

for hordes of war
tourists, gawkers
in search of

burnt-up pickup
trucks, and family
members

who want to see
where their sons
and daughters died.

NEGOTIABLES

I wish to crack
a bottle of arrack
and kick my legs
out on the verandah

before the sea
at twilight,
this pleasure,
mix of liquor

and even kisses
under whirring
fans, brought
by our soldiers

bludgeoning
villages with bombs.
They chose war,
the Tamils,

must now face
the music, hopping
on one foot
to a new master.

This is obvious, why
write poetry anymore,
or even put on a suit
or read classics?

Arrack is sweet,
and limestone
and salt and gems,
if any, in the North

will be harvested
to enjoy our southern
evenings strolling
at Unawatuna

hand in hand
under the moon;
even that Tamil
boy who lost

his mother
and father
to a misplaced
projectile,

says he must
move on,
learn a trade.
There is a new

calculus, throw
away the abacus,
Boys, the dream
has been denied.

Bend your heads
and genuflect,
we may yet
be kind

and give
you a bit
of land down
the street

from the newly-
shooted Bo
tree and
the shrine.

FIREFLIES

Condemned to live,
not for a thousand years,
but to write every day
that remains. To write
of war and its end,

of briars and desire,
of children leaping
away yet tied down
by love and memory,
circumstance.

There is no real
liberty, I have learned,
even if that spit
of Vanni and the
Jaffna Peninsula

could have served
as rump state
until kingdom come,
without friends,
how to survive

the cold peace
at meetings, become
accepted in some
LDC club ? But
Tamils ready

to invest from abroad
would have saved
Eelam from poverty.
Where shall
they house

money now?
Scarborough, Sydney,
London, Helsinki?
These are not
sandy coves or

palmyrah groves.
They carry no family
history, no stories,
but yes, in time,
every day

I shall write
until my son
and daughter turn
to me and say,
rest now,

there are new
dreams flitting
about. Let us walk
abroad and catch
the fireflies.

END NOTES

A shame and blot
on the heart, this emptiness,
yet how many of us
wander the planet
without bread or job
or some planks crossed
and nailed into a home,

while Tamils are in a tizzy
(no longer up in arms)
about civil rights and
claims to the North
and East of Lanka?
Geology makes humans
latecomers and linguists

tell us we spoke the same
proto-language before
spinning off into tribes and
nations, blathering in high
Norse or chattering
dravidian about a reed-thin
milkmaid come to drink

from the pond when
palmyrah-horsed man
spotted her long dark hair.
Not to worry, the Sri Lankan
Army has pulverized
the ancestral home of a certain
Vellupillai Prabhakaran,

in blatant disregard of poor
domestic tour operators and
the strong internal economic
push derived from in-state
tourism, but no matter, brutes
will act brutishly over such
irritants as memorials

and sources, even misguided,
of Tamil inspiration every
morning these past 30 years;
and now we read bemused
that the Jaffna Public Library

has been rebuilt. I imagine
microfilm copies of ancient

Tamil texts from across
the Bay of Bengal jostle
now for position
on the rather spacious shelves.
The ola-leafed manuscripts
in the old library were burned
of course by minister Matthew

and his orders to army fellows,
forgotten, digested in history,
unremarked except certainly
in this poem and in memories
of Tamil people who must learn
to live with the equally
meritorious Sinhala race,

part of one indivisible
and local commonwealth
administered by a rather large
Southern family, not quite
the size of the Karavas,
but almost double that band
of brothers, the Pandavas,

who saved the human race
after waging apocalypse
on the battlefield
as some survivors
of Nandikadal lagoon
describe the night and
day when shells rained

and rained without end.

UNDER BREATH

Now the war
is done, let's carry
on with our fun,
down at Galle Face

or the Oberoi,
sweet mints
to freshen up
after hot days,

and discreet
cuddles
in our rooms
before stepping

out with friends
to drink
and dance,
talk about

sacrifices
of villagers,
children fed
to artillery,

amputees
among
their first born,
and in moments

of clairvoyance
we may even
imagine
the lot of

100,000 still
in Northern
camps, while
in passing

under our breath
we whisper at first,
then raise voices
and glasses

to the crackerjack
stock market
and new
opportunities

afforded by
the visit of
the latest delegation
of Chinese.

FORBIDDEN

The chimpanzee punched
the Minister of Economy
at Dehiwela Zoo
during an informal visit
by the new ruling family
to see the lesser species
and how they manage
in captivity. A hard blow:

the next day, down
South, forestry fellows

rounded up eight hundred monkeys
who had been living easy,
according to eyewitnesses,
feasting in sugar bowls
and vegetable patches
of irate townspeople.

They came at night
and swept them up
I understand
to deposit them
deep in the jungle.
Our government
knows how to
act speedily

in humanitarian
operations
against all kinds
of foe. There shall
be no Monument
to the Missing
Chimp
of Dehiwela.

LETTER TO THE MINISTRY
OF DISASTER MANAGEMENT
AND HUMAN RIGHTS

Of course we are sad,
what do you expect,
a party every
Independence Day,

that we will succumb
to amnesia over
the course of time?

Don't worry. Children
remember what their
parents forget, and blood
unavenged, buried,
graves removed, will
receive recompense
in the same time

you raise monuments
and flags of your triumph.
How can you speak
of victory when you have
not paid for the crime of killing,
no tribute, no acknowledgment
even that civilians died?

A WALK IN THE HILLS

I want to avoid the killing field today,
hike in these hills, but not try
to imagine how rocks will tumble

when earth rumbles again. There
are saving graces to vitamins,
antioxidants, exercise, but I still

have the problem of time, stretched
rarely now as I write my way into
the fifth decade of the sojourn,

unsatisfied with faith, stinginess,
good fortune, helplessness
before the vanishing tree line.

I have always shied from placing
my body next to the bulldozer
or under the raincloud of missiles.

There is a caste called soldier,
another priest, then fool,
loquacious jester who befuddles

the king but humors him,
and in return lives. Poetry
makes nothing happen,

my favourite adage, useful
to end a scene, to say I have
done my part and written

today, far from the unmarked
and desecrated graves
of that lagoon beside

my ancient Tamilian dunes
whose dust blows and blows
and leaves no trace.

UNDIVIDED LOT

Therapeutic, to tease
out lines, untwist
thought up and down,
build stanzas no wider
than a coconut tree

on Taprobane's
coastline, garden
of delights in Latin
and Greek, Eden,
this legacy

which may yet
forgive humans
plundering
and murdering
each other

in its coves and
lagoons, beaches,
jungles. If landscapes
can swing arms
like weapons

against defilers?
There is harmony,
we know it
in the Bonsai garden.
There is peace.

We listen
to the woodpecker
pick for worms
as we walk
in early morning

to the well for water,
in Sinhala vathura,
Tamil, thani,
yet the worm
must have the right

to reply and say
to beak, to each
his own, I too shall
inherit my portion
of the garden.

FORGETTING PROCESS

Tissanaiyagam, the journalist,
has received a presidential pardon,
which absolves him of the crime
he did not commit. A minister

of the new cabinet stated
publicly that employees
of the public sector should
be trilingual and he will work

to install a system of instruction
to achieve this goal. We hear
some of the emergency
measures will be softened,

no more media monitors,
and detention without charge
can only last three months,
these are concessions, let us

not begrudge them. Shall
we say, they are goodwill
gestures from a benign
divinity who can settle

down to drink arrack
in the afternoon, no war
in the north, no journalist
union meeting the press,

even the masthead
of the *Leader* newspaper
has removed its founder's
photograph? Remember him,

bludgeoned to death
by an elite squad
on motorcycles?
His wife travels abroad

still giving untimely speeches.

CRITERIA

If you wish honour
on Remembrance Day,
there is only one litmus
test: your body must be
certified as official,
government dead.

If you had fought
for some other group

than the State,
rest assured
your gravestone
will be pulverized

and mixed with water
to make new bricks
to build a stupa
in the town which saw
you first pick up
a hand grenade,

after the school
exams (before the war)
where you failed
to meet the new
higher standard
for boys of your race.

MASTER CLASS

Reports that the Sri Lankan Army will offer lectures
on fighting insurgents to armies of the United States
and other interested powers, even if true, strike
me as unnecessary given the already existing
theory of applying overwhelming force as well as
the logical course of setting up two battle fronts

and circumscribing the rat's territory, bombing
indiscriminately, using liberal propaganda plants
in the media, that the Army will not attack safe zones
to attract rodents dressed up as civilians and to bomb
them again until they have sizzled into flames
on a spit of lagoon to which they had been swept.

There is no need for battlefield instruction, even the most
intellectually-challenged ordinary citizen has crib notes
accessible on line, available to any court interested
in further investigation of scorched earth, or close the garage
door and pump poisoned gas approach, to ridding
a confined space of movement, liberty and insurgency.

FOREIGN RAIN

It rained, rained, rained,
streets became rivers, four
people died early in Western
Province, firecrackers would not light
and the victory parade celebrating
the end of Eelam War IV washed out

while foreign meddlers
continued cackling unpleasantries
calling for investigation of war crimes,
saying hospitals, shelters, ordinary
people were bombed by order
of the high command. We all know

where to shove their words. Backbenchers
now the Labourites, and Aussies have
come round denying asylum seekers.
Forgetting is on our side, the globe
will be parried again with our latest list
of eminent persons. Look, Ban Ki Moon

has yet to establish his investigation.
The UN pulled out early, you see,
in September 2008. They too are ashamed

to sift through the dossier in case snakes
have nested there, and spirits wielding
memory sticks like staffs and divining rods.

LAND USE CHANGES

Deface gravestones with swastikas, or
write Kilroy was here, in memoriam,
shocks humans elsewhere. In Sri Lanka's
Jaffna Province, Army has broken up

headstones of Tamils who fought
in the recent war, pulverized monuments,
turned cemeteries into rubbish heaps,
surviving relatives into sleuths trying

to re-imagine possible resting
places of sons and daughters, who
may have been conscripted by rebels,
under the infamous one child offering,

and in the later stages of conflict even
a second, a human tax, for Eelam, the country
of lost hope, the Ceylonese version of the Indian
split into Pakistan, a separate state,

the only solution after earlier iterations
of apocalypse,1958,1983, now 2009, not liberated
but condemned to move ahead, to forget, to learn
the language of new street signs and tourists.

THE REAL DEAL

Like spiders, rats, viruses, Tamils have stowed
away and landed at foreign ports, invasive species
to be trapped, quarantined, in detention centers
on island properties, while escaping the Sri Lanka Option,
the source of lascivious ogling by paramilitaries,
secret services, conventional armies, and governments,
even the United Nations. So much depends of course

on the man pushing the wheelbarrow, the world´s gardener
and chief imagist, but I am falling off the reservation,
this poem does not present pure, pictorial elements
but real issues like foodstuffs and tents paid from abroad
to keep Tamils alive while locked in camps, or decisions
to pull UN reps out of Kilinochchi, to leave the city
and the Vanni open so architects of the Sri Lanka Option

could start to cast their dragnets. This poem asks the buck
to stop with you, Ban Ki Moon, that you make amends
and appoint the war crimes investigators you promised,
but you are not the only one to blame. Other than Tigers
and the Army for earlier ceasefire violations, China brought
firepower, India choked sea routes, and the West sold arms,
took them away, then tried to pressure by questioning trading

privileges, to no avail. Not to worry, some people can sleep
at night and celebrate their children's birthdays and write poems,
receive literary awards, but prizes for Sri Lankans include
posthumous recognition from international media and
human rights groups, and my own series of Oscars,
the Chutzpahs, to be given to government leaders for such
complementary measures to the fighting as denying a visa

four years running to the UN rep on extrajudicial killings,
or turning journalists away from the killing fields, and to Tigers

for earlier, deadly ruses, such as planting a boy in the kitchen
of the late President Premadasa, or the woman who exploded
before Neelan Thiruchelvam. We should not forget that Tigers
were spotted in the Middle East sharing tips on how to put on
the suicide jacket, and there is the rub of Western alarm,

but let's go back to the old adage, that two wrongs don't make
a right and refuse to accept the Chutzpah, as Marlon Brando
did once the Oscar to cast a light on trouble in the reservation,
Native American rights, but this time the people dispossessed,
raped, herded into camps, are called Tamils—not invaders
or Johnny-come-latelys—Dravidians who crossed the land bridge
when the island formed part of the subcontinent known now as
    Indian.

TRAINING

I am relieved to read that the Sri Lankan Army asked
the International Committee of the Red Cross
to train its peacekeepers on the way to UN missions
about the intricacies of international humanitarian law.

The boys need a good lesson in customs and practices
that apply abroad. Rape, for example, or shooting
captives point blank or taking no prisoners
when rebels and their families negotiate surrender

and walk out of hiding waving white flags, these
are prohibited according to an insert in the manual drafted
specially for this training, and they may well be investigated
further along, perhaps when Man plants his foot on Mars.

BLINKERED

When government pulled out
of the Ceasefire on January 16, 2008
after countless informal violations
by both sides, including aerial bombing
of Tiger properties, and bus and train
station explosions, the usual tit for tat,

this latest scorn for fruit of peacemaking
caused hardly an alarm upon the collective
snooze of the long-suffering population;
quite the contrary, on that day some thinking
Sri Lankans decided to give their spirits and
rolling eyes a rest, visiting the oculist

to have brows fitted for a hardy set of blinkers,
so they could see straight to the finish line, and
not turn back their heads to express pain
or regret when the tiger-wallah lashed his whip,
offering top wages to join the army, along
with the promise of land, securing the victory.

STAMINA

Who has the stomach or time
to read a 150-page lament,
sift through each metaphor,
accept poetry in every day
articles and speech,

everything permitted
in this particular engagement
with words and their steps?
This uncivil war has led
to the offense of insistence.

Every day the petitioner arrives
at the minister's office, early.
The secretary maintains a studied
ignorance. There are pressing
matters, Sir, cancellation

of the parade, the storm,
Twenty-four Sri lankans dead thus far,
500,000 in trouble, and you
bring us this wad of poetry paper.
Are you deranged too

with your own needs? Minister
is busy. He cannot cross certain
lines. He has his own instructions
from the last cabinet meeting
and even the executive's

consultations with parliamentarians.
There will be time for your poems
in some European country.
Here we face emergencies
still and you can imagine

how we must feel forced
to accept aid from the same
western democracies to house
our bereft people. Unfortunately,
Myanmar and Iran, our new friends,

don't appear to have well-
developed flood assistance

programs. Bring your dossier
to your senator in America,
not here, not now, never.

TWO YEARS OUT OF THIRTY

It began with rape, of women
in a Jaffna hostel, ambush of a dozen
soldiers in a convoy, then a serious rise

in the scale of response, funeral
for the soldiers in Colombo, voter lists
distributed to gangs who burnt, looted,

murdered Tamils throughout the island,
thousands of refugees, 3,000 dead.
That was 1983. In 2009, Tigers split

between North and East, weakened,
ready to be picked. Unfortunately,
300,000 civilians lived in their midst

and from January to May tens of
thousands died, tens of thousands
sported shrapnel wounds, tens of

thousands hopping still on gangrene-less
legs, and in the end, victory, exhaustion,
rebuilding under the watchful eye

of the local garrison, a reminder
that the Tamils of North and East
cannot be trusted in war or peace.

BOLLYWOOD AWARDS, COLOMBO

Dear actors, have you seen people living in tents
by the side of the road in the city of Kilinochchi?
Do you give them pots and pans to cook dhal and fry

aubergines and chillies? Do you see motion pictures
filmed in buildings and houses that remain in the center
occupied by the Army? Have you visited the fenced-off

swath rumoured to be the foundation for a more permanent
base to keep a close eye on free citizens returned
to live in their NGO-provided temporary quarters

in the city they still call home? Do you believe
that politics, this community business, not emotion,
is the root cause of disquiet in foreign lands

about the unseemly red carpet and make-believe
of Bollywood dancing in the capital Colombo
while on the same island 50,000 citizen civilians

remain in camps, and relatives, who have gone back
to live in rehabilitated Kilinochchi, beg for a new start
in life, sitting on prayer mats under tarpaulin thatches?

TO CHAMPIONS OF RECONCILIATION

Do you know how to reconcile the lot of a man,
living in a donated tent, in a city occupied by the army,
under a government that celebrates national victory,
and liberation of unfortunate civilians trodden under

the boot of devilish rebels, and continues to keep
thousands of the freed under guard in camps,
under surveillance when they return to their cities
and villages, while some analysts in the capital write
that defeated people are suspect necessarily and
require paternal supervision and safety mechanisms
while rehabilitated in professions such as sewing?

VIGIL

Keep the government guessing,
give it a meeting, not a blessing.

Let it parry with a domestic
hand-picked commission

composed of the president's
friends but insist where it hurts—

on trade, aid, weapons training—
that minorities are also human

with rights to freedoms and
property. Do not approve a family

dynasty, an inter-generational
presidency, not in the twenty-first century.

LIVING UNDER THE RAJ

Bring the gruel Matron, pour it down
the hatch, I learned how to shut up
in England, to be an effacing foreign
servant, and chose the career according
to training, bearer of the stamp, senior
clerk, but I find work goes beyond placing

a seal, or sitting in a chair under a tent
at the university ceremony. I am called
to agree to realpolitik, to haggle over
a few hundred yards, a place name,
a jingle jangle in the World Bank
assessment, to eat on occasion with

unsavoury rogues because they are
powerful hosts who derive aplomb
from birthplace, machine gun and
majority control; woe is the clause
about two thirds in favour, democracy
has no internal safeguards before

the splendour of thug-influenced
abstentions and victims
of concentrated shelling trying
to rebuild without help, aware
of eventual death, blind cause
and effect, ground water feeding

dreams still of free drinking, building
a clandestine group to throw stones
at garrison walls, assassinate an army
captain, begin the cycle again. Do not
let it happen. Build safeguards,
disband obvious signs of the Raj.

IMPOSING ORDER

Walking through detritus of gravestones pulverized,
thrown into a heap on the side of the lot surveying
what government will now build here, a monument
to victory of the unitary state, and its principal guardian,
the Sinhala soldier, worshipping at the new-made stupa
seeing his language erected on street signs while friends

and relatives come gawking in tour groups; and around
Kilinochchi and Mullaitivu, Tamil towns, in tents, soon
to be lodged in Indian-built houses, are Tamils, former
rulers, husbands, sons and daughters dead or gone
abroad, waiting to be processed, or setting up thosai
kaddais to feed visitors and soldiers, and despite

bombs and losses nursing a sullen resentment,
a necessary condition, according to think tank analysis,
to justify double-digit increase in military spending
to assure peace one year after the end of war,
a banal footnote, budget assigned to rebuild
cemeteries, squares, electric grid, houses, post

offices and water tanks of North and East equals
one percent of the amount committed to defend
the region from its most abject internal enemies,
spotted near garrisons, walking, on bicycles, crawling
out of tents to attend the mass wedding organized
at the local rehab center for former fighters in love.

MASS MARRIAGE, VAVUNIYA

What a large and dramatic idea occurred to the brigadier in charge
of rehabilitation, to organize a mass wedding to spur former Tiger

troops into formation under a different philosophy and yet appeal
to their strengths to cohere as a group not any longer in waging war

against the State but to reveal their common humanity to agree
to a public celebration of private bonds, to ensure their co-habiting

led to proper inheritance for children, access to social welfare
payments when necessary, all to the good for these members

of a herd, now in white vershtis and magenta sarees eating cake
and chatting with relatives witnessed by the Bollywood actor

Vivek Oberoi, no less, before returning to detention camps,
now two by two, respectable members of the new unitary ark,

where domestic animals gather obediently while the brigadier
sheds a tear; he told the press, he was nervous, even more so

than before his own wedding, which did not take place thankfully
under public glare and was not diminished by the splendour

of mass marriage like mass production of poultry, efficiencies
of scale, government desire to move rehabilitation forward

in one swoop, a sort of dog training in a large group; anybody
realize that marriage among truly reborn takes place between

two people and the witnesses are God and invited guests? Here,
some exceptions were made to the usual practice, no consultation

with bride or groom, whether the actor was indeed an honoured
guest, or if the brigadier should cry like a mother, or if even

fifty-three couples minded seeing their knots tied in the presence
of each other, or have Reverend Moon and other enlightened

priests of mass marriage, become advisers to Sri Lankan
military, spiritual guides to its standard operating procedure?

ON REPLACING THE SUN GOD

The Sun God disappeared from the scene in May, 2009
killed by advancing army units, not clear which brave soldier

pulled the trigger, for some reason government has kept quiet
about circumstances, but other magicians in splendid whites

are raising arms to salute on Galle Face Green's reviewing stand
troubling peace-loving citizens. They stand before armored carriers

while fighter jets fly over the head of Old Parliament at the annual
parade to celebrate the late rebirth of Dutugemunu into our democracy,

a spirit who appeared to have achieved beatitude centuries ago,
but has required one more round on his favourite hunting ground,

a touch of three kingdoms-in-one panache, obeisance of tens of
thousands marching past, and loyalty before judgment of the ruling

family which will not brook any pesky, possibly traitorous questions,
while poets must in turn choose subjects patriotically, no more kissing

under umbrellas on the Green facing crashing sea, or relaying news of
former residents of Menik Farm turned beggars on streets of Kilinochchi.

HAND WASHING

Murder cannot be hidden, bodies decompose but skeletons
remain; certainly they can be washed from beach into sea

and stripped clean by carnivorous fish yet the panel requires
just a few examples, sufficient to flesh out a theory of mass

slaughter; satellite shots will be investigated abroad and
conversations conducted with survivors of precarious boats

landing on Christmas Island or dragged into Jakarta. Scale
of killing poses a serious problem for management of disaster;

appointment of soft, suave diplomat to run damage control
at foreign ministry did not succeed. Murder will be revealed.

Macbeth is read also in Sri Lanka; it landed in the culture
before the current lot of customs inspectors; am sure

Saratchchandra contemplated translating the play if it did
not circulate already in the island like monsoon wind or ethics

which exist along with denial and chutzpah among
its inhabitants; government can throw a temper tantrum

but GSP will be linked to human rights and Ban Ki Moon
advised by his own handpicked men and eventually argument

about staring blind ahead into a bright and unitary future
while keeping North and East pressed down under army boots

will appear misguided, the world will keep reminding Colombo
that Vanni cannot remain a public jail where prisoners live

in tents and beg in thoroughfares during days supervised
by soldiers in watchtowers, on foot patrol, driving past in convoys.

LOBBING A POEM

It is almost two in the morning and not one jot of poetry
written yesterday across the page

    or
    straight
    down
    to
    hell

    however

in less than twenty-four hours a new bird will rise from
these ashes and squawk

    in rhyme

and even in the midst of excessive wrapping paper I will
find a way to remove

the present from past and into future

    poetry

and save myself a lift ticket to ride back up the mountain
top, step

into the foot impression on Adam's Peak, jangle keys at
Heaven's Gate,

and there is the rubber-rub rub, Sri Lanka will introduce
itself in most

unseemly fashion into Molotov cocktail-party impolite
poetry writing.

JUSTICE (POETIC)

Why don't you come back
for a toddy and sunshine,

a glass of arrack, a walk
on the beach without fear

of bombers or police? . . .
Well, not quite, one still

cannot hold hands or
kiss, and it is reasonable

to think you will be
impounded at the airport

and driven to the poetic
assessment building, sixth

floor where toughest lines
are hammered into iambs

before throwing all syllabic
waste out the window.

INHERITANCE

There is no rule written in an enormous ledger by an acolyte angel
that says a poet will write every day until death. The uncivil war will end

according to absence of such dictate when humors start to break down
cellular walls and cancer spreads overcoming defences of heart, lungs,

kidneys, gut, brain, in no particular order, as aforementioned parts
succumb to constant hammering of shells, fits of barking orders to kill,

and distant turning away from disaster, beating breasts, while asking
focus groups, how can we intervene in a sovereign nation, does this

particular wilful disregard for human life meet your standard, fellow
citizens and friends? Pure fantasy. Nobody consulted the man in Peoria

or the soothsayer shuffling along to the bead shop on Main Street. There
was no attempt to interfere with ordinary irritations of Western peoples

living in their democracies, or Chinese factory workers assembling sound
cards. Father or politburo know best whether to donate or lend fighter jets

in return for port concession and road-building, forest-felling contracts and
much more promised also to the other great power of the Indian Ocean,
    but

how to determine the amount any government can sell in order to kill
    in peace,
to eliminate its cancer with a terrifying dose of radiation, to keep the
    ground hot

and de-mine it slowly over decades while population dies off or
    sympathizers abroad
tire of protest marches on anniversary days. Human societies are slow to
    heal,

nurse resentments over decades and centuries. Welcome to hurt passed
  down
to children and grandchildren, to unpaid crimes, suppressed anger, cold war.

UNSETTLED

for Sanjana

Let us embrace the brute truth, the one
we cannot hide away in dreams or write

on a scrap of cardboard and stick
in the leaves of a book we will abandon

when nobody shall be left to care for us
or for our tombstones; my father got back

to Jaffna in time to visit his mother's grave
before his heart stopped. My heart races

even faster now, so many deaths which merit
remembrance, headstones pulverized

in the Vanni, all these relatives weighing
scales, how many Southern war widows

and how many in the north, two sides the same,
yet my friend says I am half-blind, I cannot

see brother and sister but love my neighbor
and grew up in the multicultural dream,

not deferred but effaced, alive once now dead,
to be salvaged still when current generations

pass away in the slowly rising waters, and new
kinds of men without memory, concentrated

in daily living and homage to their gods, turn
over and out of their mothers' loins to be born.

SRI LANKAN WINTER

Outside London's Dorchester
night falls in wet snowflakes, biting
wind, black men holding placards
calling for Mahinda's head.

Inside the hotel, president in white
vershti surrounded by apostles,
bodyguards, yes men, receives
word that his sermon will not

be heard at the Oxford Union.
Poor man, he can't control
his message outside the island,
his kingdom extends only

to familiar shorelines, Galle Face,
Dondra Head, and the new colonies
of Jaffna, Mullaitivu, and the rest
of Eelam as well, at this time.

A SCENE: JAFFNA

When comedy becomes tragedy
and the show lasts over generations
the audience, exhausted, cross-
eyed, bored, astonished, programs
in hand like paper airplanes, should
say bygones be damned and walk

through the proscenium into theater
of the absurd where soldiers spread
putty over furniture, unsupervised
by a nanny, and poor men still ride
bicycles home in Jaffna's evening
while vans without license

plates make house inquiries, and
essayists, in the capital and abroad,
write obsessively about headlights
and other props to capture the effects
of disappearance and other pops
through the trap door of night.

UNEQUAL RIGHTS

Thou shalt not
fails to apply

in the serendipitous
north of the isle.

Here fate and
destiny are shuffled

in the pack
by a master shark

who has no qualms
in stripping water

of prehistoric fish
spouting still murky

ideas from distant
pasts of Europe and

America—where
freedom of assembly

and right to title
of land that once

belonged to family
have been seconded

to high security zones
and their guardians

of liberty, the national
and venerable army.

CYCLING

Periyapappa used to listen
to the Tamil Service
on a transistor radio
all afternoon, resting

in his single bed, or
at a desk, during
his long retirement.
He lived into his 90s

for the purpose
of this poem, I don't
recall now whether death
took him a few years shy

of that magic number,
it does not matter
my friend says; you
talk of leaving Sri Lanka

at eight but it seems
to me you are living
there still, peeling
rambutans, diving

into the sea while
motorbikes surround
your editor-in-chief
at the intersection

before murdering him,
leaving you and a motley
family, liberal, gentle,
educated to let the fly

buzz in its orbit, snake
slide through the grass
to fulfill its role in the play,
eat rats and battle

the mongoose, trap
Man only when he walks

unaware through the night
and steps on a mine that rears

and bites his leg or hand.
Let us find antidotes fast,
stanch venom, suck
it out or cut off the limb

as necessary, at least Man
will live to hop about his garden
and eat mangos, rambutans,
supervise his property, listen

to the transistor radio
until death moves him
along to the next battlefield
or garden of delights.

FLOWN AWAY

This minced meat, keema
mixed with rice and peas
and a cup of milk tea,

Pakistan brought home
with raita and good
company at Shant Cottage,

Kent, where the proprietor
asked me to focus—
on the tips of leaves,

birds' nests in high
branches, where new
blackbirds will fly—not

in roots preserved
in the jewelry box,
shaved nails, hair locks,

that the muddy river
and its squealing fowl
no longer form a part

of the English body,
free, yet pleased
to eat this meal,

to share a bit of Pakistan
with a prodigal son
who stopped by to chat

far from his island
home, Ceylon,
rubbed off the map.

NOTHING LEFT

There is nothing left but poetry
said the farmer to his cows

gone mad. There is nothing
left but poetry said the president

to advisors as he plotted
how to stay in his palace

after the people voted him out.
There is nothing left but poetry

said the man who ordered
Lasantha killed as he faced

the journalist's ghost every
feast day. There is nothing left

but lines hammered into a verse,
said Yeats about Connolly and Pearse.

There is nothing left unsaid
here, elsewhere and in poetry,

said the critic to his class. Yet
we must study the classics and

write poetry. Nothing else remains,
nothing else said the poet to himself.

THE DYKE BROKE

The dyke broke, sandbags crumbled
and water flowed into my computer
washing away all the pictures and poems,
and now that I am dry and facing

a new bed I wonder how shall I nourish
the seeds you furnish without returning
to the waters to salvage some instrument
that kept its hide like these tablas tapping

the morning on the Tamil Service. Surely,
a man is not a cat, that he must make
amends with his life, prepare the bed
with his heart and memory? Make it new,

his maestro remarked. Renew, renew
chimed the songbirds in chorus.

THE RIGHT TO RESPOND

NGO: The numbers do not
add up. Census says 430,000
people resided in the Vanni
mid-2008. A year later, 290,000
are shepherded by the Army
into "welfare centers" where
one hundred men, boys, girls,
women shared one latrine, but
that is another dirty subject;
we are speaking here of brute
numbers and mass disappearance.

Gov't: I understand
Tamil Net will jump to spread
the pernicious bleeding
heart report from those pesky
fellows at Channel 4,
so we must follow
our Leader and enact
his plan to send teams
to like-minded, non-aligned
countries to show how
governments can eliminate

terror, following our way
or the highway, of no return,
but we won't use that crude
phrase. We believe we are

among friends here
in the poem without a need
to camouflage. Yet, we must
practice to win the diplomatic
battle now in the third and
fourth worlds where we
are very much at home.

CLIMATE-INDUCED

Plantain leaves, steaming yellow
rice, katta sambol, seer fish,

passion fruit, the island's culinary
pleasures I think of first, batting

then for a day, stopping for lunch
and tea, but this strain of poetry

has been sidelined, a war
won and lost, rewriting of history,

yet the latter may not be
necessary, building of

monuments to the bullet
near the sea, or the various

stupas popping up by kovils,
or replacing them quietly.

The waters of the Bay
of Bengal are rising steadily.

AT YOUR SERVICE

Islanders always like to baila,
party, party, nibble the ear

whispering, pump themselves
with arrack and go courting

on the Green, but in these
holidays at year's end

dedicated to forgetting
the war and all those gadflies

buried in graves, some families
mourn their heroes away

from the headlights' glare
of vans without license plates

that remain in service waiting
to be summoned when necessary.

OVERSEEING THE FARM

Planning a visit home is not easy
for a Tamil returning to Jaffna. First,
he needs to fly into the international
airport at Katunayake and pass
through customs like any traveler.

He may be asked to step into
a back room, to answer why

he carries the *Economist*
in hand luggage, or stickers
from the World Wildlife campaign

to save the tiger, given that
such animals have not been spotted
on the island in thousands of years,
if indeed they ever sauntered through
the wild grass or paddy fields.

He may be grilled about
family members in Wellawatte,
and what career he pursues
in the Scarborough, Ontario refuge
where wild and liberal creatures found

a home before conservatives took
over in Ottawa; he may be whisked
through secondary, and into a waiting
vehicle for a fast ride to the upstairs room
at CID headquarters where he will meet

his guide, his helper, who will say,
come friend, the campaign is lost,
give me a few names of laggards,
dreamers still in the foreign networks.
We must root out the germ.

Human beings have almost
eradicated polio, why not this
virulent, regional strain called
Eelam? Unfortunate, the cricketer
who failed a dope test,

and the others charged
with fixing matches, and
the Tamil policemen, who trained
in the hot sun for weeks to march
in the Victory parade for Eelam War IV,

told they cannot, on orders
of the President's security detail.
What the hell, machan,
in paradise only Man is vile, said
the preacher who visited the island

in ancient times. Now we are renewed,
climate savvy, the A-9 Highway
is open to tourists beyond
Elephant Pass, but not yet, without
permission, to returning Tamils,

Hambantota boasts a deep water
port, and all our teenagers will
receive mandatory training
in military arts, which should help
them run animal farms in the far North.

WEARING THIN

These smart, smug,
schmucks who believe
9/11 gave then license

to stamp out restive
minorities, labeling
every kid and his mum

siblings and progenitors
of terrorists, gypsy
population

of the Vanni
game for shelling
in hospital, tent,

on the road, revealed
now by trophy camera,
cell phone, drone,

Sri Lanka's Killing Fields
requiring a worldwide
publicity campaign

for the Rajapakse boys
who must be perplexed
by the extreme foreign

exchange cost
of their millennial
triumph. The world

will forget they bet,
not realizing
that Simon Wiesenthal

is a living concept,
and even the patience
of the United States—
about lack of
unmonitored access
to the North,

persistence
of prisoners hidden
out of sight,

extrajudicial
killing in peace time,
all the blanks

in the nation's
accounting books,
is wearing out.

PRESCIENT

When Lasantha wrote the editorial that predicted
his imminent assassination he suggested the civil war
would turn steadily uglier, then move inwards,

as a lizard searching for its tail, insidious in the way
each institution begins to lose its independence,
the machinery of the ruling family greasing every

Tom, Dick and Banda—forgive my allusion to white
rulers of a more genteel if not innocent nursery school—
this forsaken Ceylonese child has turned monstrous now

in the eyes of Whitehall and Ottawa's Parliament Hill,
betters going wild about pressures in Canberra to present
a bold brief on behalf of human rights and investigation

of war crimes as Commonwealth heads prepare to meet,
while on the island rival thugs, from within the all-powerful
ruling group, battle over drug routes, a parliamentary seat.

CHERAN

He is writing history, where he lives, when he travels,
to Denmark, Singapore, Tamil Nadu, Toronto. Edward Said
wrote about Palestinians, Rudramoorthy Cheran, Tamils.

News that my friend has suffered a mild heart attack
does not surprise me. His muscle has been strained
for more than thirty years. From the *Saturday Review*

where he reported first days of rebellion in Jaffna
to more recent sociological study and dramatic writing,
the man, as scientist and poet, has let emotions hang

on strings strummed to a tabla's beat. Wordsmiths
for Tamilians are as good as our instruments
and words are always enhanced by music. I recall

when we met in 1987 at the International Centre
for Ethnic Studies on Kynsey Terrace in Colombo,
where I moved as a kid when the house was home

and not yet a center dedicated to resolving differences,
the wounds of the 1983 "Riots" were still very fresh,
and enthusiasm for resolution of long-standing

grievances strong, and nobody thought
we would allow democracy to fall into tyranny.
Neelan had not yet crossed the hairs of a Tiger,

nor even Premadasa, but the Indian Army were
landing in Jaffna, and resistance came soon after
that brief spring during which Cheran and I smoked

a cheroot and spoke poetry tinged with sadness
still for the murders of Black July and later,
on another visit, the suicide of Sivaramani,

whom we translated before the light
of an oil lamp in a thosai kaddai and thought
that, now we live abroad, let us recognize

at least that our spirits will not present passports
and our children, whom we could not imagine
then, would wander about our new homes and one day

think that to be Tamil is to be well-prepared to write
the essay on expulsion from the garden, and to feed, dream
and compose that other promise too: the right of return.

DEFENDING THE COUNTRY

They cry foul in that cauldron
of a news room, saying these
human rights defenders
are traitors, publishing

their names and photographs,
inciting fears of death
squads preparing to drive
white vans to their residences.

The warning by the UN Human
Rights Commissioner to protect
witnesses is welcome, quixotic.
How will her office stop disappearances

when government has rejected
the resolution, said it will push back
reconciliation, which I presume to mean
more islanders vanished, bloodshed,

people living in fear and loathing,
keeping quiet or moving out,
accompanied to the airport
by diplomats from a friendly mission,

leaving their homes to caretakers,
a new life abroad for champions
of human rights at home? And
for those who stay, negotiating

protections, waiting for
a post-midnight call
by an elite team of assassins,
like the ones who shot

prisoners at Nandikadal,
stopping motorbikes
in the intersection
to beat Lasantha to death,

dressed in black with black
glasses, or as drivers
of white vans, in assorted
civilian garb, ordinary

people working
a second job at night,
disappearing themselves
into the morning rush.

OFF THE FIELD

In the end we have only ourselves to pick up from the grass,
the bed, the gymnasium floor. The dead will have their say
in dreams, and fond ones too, how the boy used to laugh

when chasing the ball on Duplication Road, or the girl back
in the village, shyly accept the glance of her neighbor's son,
by the well, over a garden wall, the victims, the left behind

after the tsunami or the shelling without end, abroad,
processed, rebuilding their lives in the company of
Australians or Canadians, new people, while the distant war

on its nightly visit to parents, single or a pair, does not curse
the kid born away, who loves the latest fad on satellite radio
and the girl in his class who sports an infectious laugh.

EXECUTED SUMMARILY

The Sri Lanka Killing Fields documentaries remind us of what
took place while we manned barricades, carrying posters
and placards, shouting in the evening off Robson Square,

on Parliament Hill, in our far-away democracies. We are told
that the rest of the world, the United Nations, just wanted
the war to finish, inevitably, with government victory

while hoping that the largest possible number of hapless civilians
crouched in bunkers, running from shell to shell, would live
to prosper again. Forty thousand or more died while survivors

166

languished in detention camps, released now to live on scraps
without jobs in a vast territory full of monuments to the victory,
army camps, soldiers manning intersections, running investments,

rebuilding projects in Chinese and Indian hands, and stupas
erected beside kovils, new street names, and prohibitions
on singing a certain national song in Tamil, a mild suggestion

to help make peace palatable, that Tamils will be allowed
to sing in Tamil, even this remains to be adopted, yet how
to keep colleagues at work, friends informed when repressions

elsewhere have claimed their due rights, inevitably,
to the headlines. In Homs, Syria, Marie Colvin was targeted
again by a government shell, this time she died.

Back in 2001 she shouted that she was a journalist, while
walking towards government forces in the Sri Lankan theatre,
and a grenade tore out her eye. She survived, bore witness

to the war which in its moments of final resolution did
not allow entry even to the Red Cross, to pick up wounded,
deliver surgical supplies. We know now that captured

or surrendering fighters, as well as some civilians hiding
in bunkers, Tamils, babies and old people, whomever
soldiers found mopping up, were executed summarily.

ACCOUNTING FOR CIVILIANS

Nonplussed means surprised
and confused, says the Oxford
online, but the editors add,

almost as an afterthought,
wearily, resigned, that in recent
North American usage the word

has taken on the opposite
sense, as in unperturbed.
This variant does not form part

of standard English, they claim.
Who will determine the fate
of nonplussed? Who shall

write the new standards?
Every afternoon outside
47th Street and First

placards are out
screaming nonplussed
about the latest caving

in of the United Nations
before murders of innocents,
unperturbed, in far-away fields.

THREE DEATHS,
ANOTHER DISAPPEARED

Risks reporters take,
crossing the border
from Turkey, up
a mountain path
on a horse sparking
his allergy, Shadid
entering Syria.

In Colombo,
Lasantha drove
his car to a light
where a team
of assassins
on motorcycles
bludgeoned him.

In Homs, Marie,
blinded in an eye
from an army grenade
in the Vanni succumbed
to aerial bombing
of her dwelling. These
are circumstances

of three deaths, one
accidental. How
to characterize
asthma, a risk
unabetted by Man,
lots cast on his body,
destiny? How to know

the limits of what
he or his family
would endure, his wife,
infant son? Lasantha
left children, Prageeth,
the cartoonist, as well.
He disappeared two years

ago, can't include him
yet among the confirmed
dead, all of them giving
us stories of casualties
in wars to break the hold
of the state, its exclusive
propriety of liberty.

DAWN

Write what you feel
sitting down in the street
while the tank rolls

and stops inches
from your feet.
Write the boy's words

in confidence
by the fire, burning
instructions to spread

the revolt while
drinking a tea
with condensed milk.

Write the thoughts
of a senior man,
judge, engineer,

principal, when
the law made
his language

a lesser evil,
a private tongue.
Write the defusing

of a grenade
lobbed into the parlor
while the family cowered

in a garden pit. Then
speak to the palm trees
and the paddy birds

about the whistling
sound of a missile,
the rat-a-tat-tat

of a machine gun.
Oh, sorry, let me
try once more:

the beauty
of dawn over
the jungle canopy.

KILLER REPRESENTATIVE

I am assembling the scene, a local hood
and his gang come to a Christmas Eve

gathering at a beach hotel, want to dance
with foreign women, see a bloke from town

trotting high with a blonde, but when
they ask for a spin, are spurned, although

they are hotshots in the area, their chief
an elected representative; they have guns

and knives in their pockets, or placed
discreetly on their reserved table, and

they tear a woman from her boyfriend,
cutting her up and him, then shooting.

Government in a dither, keeping press
at bay, we cannot have these stories

displayed in the West where similar
incidents take place in the most respected

capitals, says another representative,
and the perpetrators have been booked,

are under investigation, although the head
of the local governing council has been known

to kill in the past but nobody is sure who can,
or will, introduce historical evidence.

A FISHERMAN TESTIFIES

I learned from Sri Lanka
to go overboard, to flounder
in the deep ocean

while Navy sailors beat
me with sticks, and cut
my nets, and round me up

as the country's diplomats
meet my Indian representatives
with elaborate denials

of mistreatment
on the high and most
domestic seas.

I want to feed
my wife and children,
return to Tamil Nadu

with my catch. I have
not been re-schooled
as a farmer

or an errand boy.
Will the United Nations
take up my case?

The International
Criminal Court?
My Chief Minister

protests and protests
but the Center is deaf
and keeps speaking

with the Devil.
How can we calm
his temperature,

cool the beast,
teach the Tyrant
that he cannot stifle

Tamils beyond
the nautical limits
of the Sri Lankan island?

THE ISLAND ABSTAINS

The decision by the Democratic Socialist Republic
of Sri Lanka to abstain from the General Assembly vote
calling for an end to violence in Syria, and stepping down
of its president, cannot be accused of inconsistency,

given the island republic's wish to continue importing
Iranian oil, serve tea at official Syrian garden parties,
and its pummel-the-minority most successful
bombing strategy. that just three years ago seemed

to be the talk of Colombo town. Unfortunately,
the government faces a resolution of its own,
upcoming in Geneva, and perhaps the abstaining
route indicates a not unsubtle wish that it may go

unperceived in the noise of those who said yes
or no. Some of us noticed, however, the way
Lankan diplomats exercised the popular will and
we present evidence here in the court of poetry.

WE ARE RESOLVED

Sri Lanka is small
but the government
thinks big, always has;
since independence

its growth rate
in ministries and
delegations the envy
of Asia, and now

defeat of
the resolution
the charge of
fifty-two valiant diplomats

whose arrack flows
in hospitality suites
at night, while
mornings are spent

chatting about contracts,
coal-fired plants,
fish meal, everything
as long as the other

party speaking
does the needful,
as we say
in our language,

to save the gentleman's
agreement, the brilliant
and home-grown war
on terror strategy

and abstains, or much
better for later tabling
and closing of reports,
votes against.

FROM THE HOLD

I don't merit praise. Who am I to suggest
inventing the West Moon for the Lankan

imagination, or that one day a Tamil child
will rise from fires to claim the rights

of his tribe? Boat people, Tamils,
flee Serendip. Governing criminals

are stopping the motors, forcing
families to remain in their island prison.

Who shouts in the Hague,
on Downing Street, outside

the White House? More Tamils,
defenders of human rights, liberals,

Don Quijotes, while the Murderer,
and Jail Keep, licks his mutton chops.

RIGHT WORD FOR BOAT

To replace "boat" you propose ark,
which appears quaint in 2012,
but for Tamils getting on board,
strangely right, the chance

for new life, doves flying on
the other side of the Indian Ocean

to Christmas Island, where
beside large numbers

of endemic plant and animal
species, island uninhabited until
the nineteenth century, and still
only a thousand five hundred

year-round-settlers, Australia
built a holding pen, detention
facility, with 800 beds for offshore
registration of would-be immigrants,

asylum seekers. The Ark meets
Christmas says the headline
in my scrapbook documenting
family journeys in skiffs,

dinghys, lifeboats, trawlers,
each vessel a dream of new life,
not the dangers of running
aground, sea swallows.

EXTRA TIME

The latest news
from the Family-run,
once independent island,

is the appointment
of a presidential committee
to decide upon which

recommendations to adopt
regarding the erstwhile
ethnic question,

subsumed since
into the unitary enterprise
of the war-fighting, now

North and East-occupying,
government dedicated
to paying appropriate attention

to the international human
rights lobby and European
and American states.

Nothing like a committee
to push the football away,
like the many formed

and dissolved
in the past without
achieving laws,

but which gained time
for the Family
to work and play.

THE WRITER FIGHTER

Have you become
a lance corporal,
wing commander,

lieutenant, private,
sergeant, major general?
Or are you a writer

transporting yourself
into trenches to wield
a saber against a vague

menace, bespectacled,
sitting at a computer,
trying to finish

his latest report
on the war
without witnesses

that went wrong
somehow because
the witnesses

and warriors
snapped photos
on cell phones

and sent them
to scribes
composing

on computers
eternal odes
to mere privates

in trenches,
launching projectiles
from bazookas,

following orders,
not responsible
for blood baths

beyond gun sites,
in no man's land,
no fire zones?

SEPARATE THE CHILD

Where did you grow your politics?
Thousands of palmyra stalks,
fronds and fruit blown off
in aerial straffing, bombs heaved
on houses and men on bicycles,
rocket launchers, grenades,
human Tiger explosions,
civilians sandwiched
in no man's land, Nandikadal.
This is a partial answer.

My father's friends, sired
by all ethnicities, led the society,
graduated from missionary schools
into the Ceylon Civil Service,
following merit-based examinations,
became an impeccable class
of administrators lost forever,
our children condemned
to mono-lingual ignorance.
This is a partial answer.

Betrayal of my father and
his Ceylonese big tent philosophy,
in parliament, scuttling appointment
to Islamabad claiming he opposed

Muslims, defending Sinhala Buddhist
chauvinism, critiquing foreign evaluations
of government war methods
I read, with bitterness, one of his
English-educated, urbane friends.
This is a partial answer,

My mother who suffered gossips
assigning madness to my brother's autism,
who said father had flown too high
in the landscape, who kept quiet
in Colombo, no flaunting of Tamil,
no license plates, and living
in the right neighborhood where
thugs would not visit, even
in the 60s, two years after 1958.
This is a partial answer,

and I can write and write
rubbing the glass, summoning
glimpses of the depths
of my sadness and scorn. How
could the Tigers have killed
their own, that schmuck
Athulathmudali, like his political
ancestor, albeit from
a different party, Bandaranaike,
a disgrace to the Oxford Union,

as defense minister
full of blood lust at home
where the good drink
scotch until they keel over.
War time, baby, all's fair
as long as the Tamil civilians
are kept hostage—1983—
or have moved to their homelands

under the tutelage of the Tiger cult:
the final solution, a partial answer.

A break in the dykes built
by forced labor, Tigers split
into North and East, traitors
by the dozen, turned ministers
in the only one hundred-strong
cabinet known to Man to leave us
with the glorious peace,
300,000 civilians left in Jaffna
guarded by 100,000 soldier Sinhalese;
while the current criminal lot

of rulers and their representatives
abroad, followed on after the fabled
Kadirigamar who aspired to become
the first Tamil prime minister,
bumped off for a cause, murder
unexplained, unprosecuted, without
settling on terms with Prabhakaran
who martyred his own people
and Indran who left the island
as a child, writing now this history.

NANDIKADAL

I did not realize I would become
sensitive at fifty-one, an age one
would think of fifty projects
to occupy the mind, not one of
which implied missing a daughter
blind, or trying to hip hop through

the weeds to spot an egret
fishing, or the stuffed corpse
of a Tamil scaring birds away
from the lagoon, which will
remain sacred burial ground
for dreams, a nation, spring
poetry up in every generation
to come until thy will be done.

HAPPINESS BLUES, SRI LANKA

I don't know what to say, my friend,
I have some blues that don't seem right,
too light and fancy free, happiness
and all that putty you poke and pat,

grinning silly, but love is the matter
with me, I have plenty and I want
to start sharing the bounty. How lucky
can a man be, used to melancholy

and raving at the Moon about family
buried by the lagoon, who will
catch the drift along with snowflakes
in this far Northern and European town

that tried to make peace back
in the viper-ridden Vanni and failed;
yet somehow, miraculously, cousins
survived and are making their way
out of the jungle, heads held high;

and throughout the planet
family is saying this effort

to settle foundation stones
of our piece of earth will continue

until the end of time; so nobody
should rest on laurels, or dream
of bitter death, happiness
has me up tonight, generous

and lively. Are you ready
for a roll? A reading
about uncivil fools who think
blood can be washed away,

bones buried in the sand,
that everybody will forget
how one hand clapped
and white vans set off

to prowl? No, my friends,
this happiness will not
be shovelled into the back
seat or stuffed with cloth

down its throat or peppered
in the eyeballs. It will not expire
before midnight. We are
about to play—the crowd

is eager and shouting—
a post-midnight set, happiness
blues, after the reckoning,
the counting of the dead.

TAMIL RESURRECTION

Am standing outside,
don't know how to get in.
Am standing outside,
sun burning my skin.

Am standing outside
'til evening drops,
night falls. Don't know
how to make night

rise or evening
take flight. I write
four beat blues,
shuffle in my shoes.

I am free deliciously
to sing up the tree.
I will land in Heathrow
or via satellite

on the Moon
and beyond.
I am irresponsible,
a Tamil, a dreamer,

a boy. I am alive
still and will not
die off like a tune.
I will sing

for my supper
and school.
I wear the colors
in case I run

into another fool
who lives by
old rules. I believe
in marbles

and tuck shops,
spicy fish.
I am English,
Tamil, and Welsh

for the bards.
I am your friend
in chapter and verse,
a poet who cannot

be shut off
like a spout.
I am ground water
and my source

is deep, hidden,
No hound dog
or metal detector
can sniff me out.

I promise not
to explode
but hear my song.
Give me

a deed
to the land
where
I am buried.

HOWLING

What shall I do, living
in Peru, with this report
of systemic failure

in UN monitoring
in Sri Lanka, how
bureaucrats drove away

from the disaster to come,
buried hard-earned stats
about civilian deaths

and allowed themselves
to be brow-beaten,
harassed, shouted

into silence while
40,000 or more
humans died, mostly

from battering shells
rained from fighter jets?
I belong to the family

of nations. I have
a vote in one
democracy,

dream of serving
humanity,
in the Secretariat

of the United Nations.
of inside influence,
reform within, extracting

the worm, of keeping
a job close to the Secretary
General, speaking

into his ear, saying
fix your flank, Man,
souls are howling.

WITNESS

I write my life
morning to night.
I have no other tale
to relate. Paddy

and palmyrah,
chillies screaming
in early light, crying
girl running loose

through grass, smoke
from the straight
hit where field gulfed
and lovers, clasped,

rolled into the pit.
Bah humbug your war
without observers.
We are singing now

over the earth;
the Sun is out; Ban
Ki Moon has seen
evidence

island potentates
cannot hide.
This poem bears
witness.

READY TO MOVE

We are Mayans.
We are Tamils.
We are Armenians.
We are Germans
who lived once
in Poland.

We are Burkinabes
stuck in Abidjan.
Somalians
in Maine and
Massachusetts.
We are witnesses

to the only truth
worth repeating:
have a bag
of essentials
holy book,
toothbrush,

a fresh set
of clothes, ready
to put on your back
when historical
conditions change
suddenly.

RECONSTRUCTION

Going south again with mixed feelings,
you say, I relate. Watching the snaps

of a cousin's wedding, sister present,
guests in dapper suits, intense heat,

contrasts that shaped me, and to think
I did not know she was to marry,

that I missed Prasanth's sixtieth,
memorial masses of all the recent

dead. As for those from genocide
who wait for votive candles

and the bereaved unable to assemble
in the Vanni to mourn, I join you

here, scratching another poem
into the retaining wall

of a house, bruised, open
to the sky, standing still.

Indran Amirthanayagam writes poetry and essays in English, Spanish, French and Portuguese. His works include *The Splintered Face, Ceylon R.I.P., El Infierno de Los Pájaros, El Hombre que Recoge Nidos, Sol Camuflado, La Pelota del Pulpo* and *The Elephants of Reckoning,* which won the 1994 Paterson Poetry Prize. His poetry has appeared in numerous magazines and journals throughout the world. He has also published translations of Mexican poets Manuel Ulacia and Jose Eugenio Sanchez. He is a diplomat in the United States Foreign Service. He writes a blog on poetry at http://indranamirthanayagam.blogspot.com.